WHO DO WE
CHOOSE TO BE?

Tao of Physics
Fritjof Capra
YouTube

WHO DO WE CHOOSE TO BE?

FACING REALITY
CLAIMING LEADERSHIP
RESTORING SANITY

MARGARET J. WHEATLEY

Berrett–Koehler Publishers, Inc.
a BK Life book

Berrett-Koehler Publishers, inc.
1333 Broadway, Suite 1000
Oakland, CA 94612-1921
Tel: (510) 817-2277   Fax: (510) 817-2278   www.bkconnection.com

Ordering Information

Quantity sales. Special discounts are available on quantity purchases by corporations, associations, and others. For details, contact the "Special Sales Department" at the Berrett-Koehler address above.

Individual sales. Berrett-Koehler publications are available through most bookstores. They can also be ordered directly from Berrett-Koehler: Tel: (800) 929-2929; Fax: (802) 864-7626; www.bkconnection.com

Orders for college textbook/course adoption use. Please contact Berrett-Koehler: Tel: (800) 929-2929; Fax: (802) 864-7626.

Orders by U.S. trade bookstores and wholesalers. Please contact Ingram Publisher Services, Tel: (800) 509-4887; Fax: (800) 838-1149; E-mail: customer.service@ingrampublisherservices.com; or visit www.ingrampublisherservices.com/Ordering for details about electronic ordering.

Distributed to the U.S. trade and internationally by Penguin Random House Publisher Services.

Berrett-Koehler and the BK logo are registered trademarks of Berrett-Koehler Publishers, Inc.

Printed in Canada

Berrett-Koehler books are printed on long-lasting acid-free paper. When it is available, we choose paper that has been manufactured by environmentally responsible processes. These may include using trees grown in sustainable forests, incorporating recycled paper, minimizing chlorine in bleaching, or recycling the energy produced at the paper mill.

Production management: Michael Bass Associates
Book design: Canace Pulfer
Cover/jacket design: Margaret Wheatley and Canace Pulfer
Cover photograph: West Temple, Zion National Park Utah by Margaret Wheatley
"Energy 1" and "Energy 2" paintings, pp. 148 and 153: Phil Robbins, used with permission
All other interior photos: Margaret Wheatley
Author photo: Filiz Telek

Library of Congress Cataloging-in-Publication Data
Names: Wheatley, Margaret J., author.
Title: Who do we choose to be? : facing reality, claiming leadership, restoring sanity / Margaret J. Wheatley.
Description: First edition. | Oakland : Berrett-Koehler Publishers, [2016] | Includes index.
Identifiers: LCCN 2017002226 | ISBN 9781523083633 (pbk.)
Subjects: LCSH: Leadership.
Classification: LCC HD57.7 .W4563 2016 | DDC 658.4/092—dc23
LC record available at https://lccn.loc.gov/2017002226

First Edition
22 21 20 19 18 17   10 9 8 7 6 5 4 3 2

Dedication

For Pema Chödrön who, with pure insight and compassion, led me onto the path of warriorship and continues to guide me ever deeper

and

For the Warriors for the Human Spirit who have joined me in training so we might learn how best to serve this time

The Warriors arise
when the people need protection

We don't have to wait for some grand utopian future. The future is an infinite succession of presents, and to live now as we think human beings should live, in defiance of all that is bad around us, is itself a marvelous victory.

— Howard Zinn, historian

What This World Needs

This world does not need more entrepreneurs.
This world does not need more technology breakthroughs.
This world needs leaders.

We need leaders who put service over self, who can be
steadfast through crises and failures, who want to stay
present and make a difference to the people, situations, and
causes they care about.

We need leaders who are committed to serving people, who
recognize what is being lost in the haste to dominate, ignore,
and abuse the human spirit.

We need leaders because leadership has been debased
as those who take things to scale or are first to market or
dominate the competition or develop killer apps. Or hold onto
power by constantly tightening their stranglehold of fear until
people are left lifeless and cowering.

We need leaders now because we have failed to implement
what was known to work, what would have prevented or
mitigated the rise of hatred, violence, poverty, and ecological

destruction. We have not failed from a lack of ideas and technologies. We have failed from a lack of will. The solutions we needed were already here.

Now it is too late. We cannot solve these global issues globally. We can see them clearly. We can understand their root causes. We have evidence of solutions that would have solved them. But we refused to compromise, to collaborate, to persevere in resolving them as an intelligent, creative species living on one precious planet.

Now it's up to us, not as global leaders but as local leaders. We can lead people to create positive changes locally that make life easier and more sustainable, that create possibility in the midst of global decline.

Let us use whatever power and influence we have, working with whatever resources are already available, mobilizing the people who are with us to work for what they care about.

As President Teddy Roosevelt enjoined us:

Do what you can, with what you have, where you are.

OPENING

1. THE ARROW OF TIME

Everything Has a Beginning, a Middle, and an End

2. IDENTITY

Living Systems Change in Order to Preserve Themselves

3. INFORMATION

It's Better to Learn Than Be Dead

4. SELF-ORGANIZATION

Order for Free

5. PERCEPTION

What You See Is All You Get

OPENING

Let your wisdom as a human being connect with the power of things as they are.

— Chögyam Trungpa, Buddhist teacher

An Invitation to the Nobility of Leadership

It is possible, in this time of profound disruption, for leadership to be a noble profession that contributes to the common good. It is possible, as we face the fearful complexity of life-destroying problems, to experience recurring moments of grace and joy. It is possible, as leaders of organizations, communities, and families, to discover deep and abiding satisfaction in our work if we choose not to flee or withdraw from reality. It is possible to find a path of contribution and meaning if we turn our attention away from issues beyond our control and focus on the people around us who are yearning for good leadership and engage them in work that is within reach. It is possible to use our influence and power to create *islands of sanity* in the midst of a raging destructive sea.

——

So much is possible if we consciously and wisely choose how best to step forward as leaders for this time.

——

This is a book that offers a path for leaders to engage well and sanely with the destructive dynamics of this time that now manifest at every level, from individual to organizational to global. We enter the path by bravely facing reality, willing to see with clarity and discernment where we are and how we got here. We seek to understand the forces at work that created this present world, not the one we have spent long years laboring to create, but a world that increasingly harms most and benefits scant few, a world stubbornly spiraling toward self-destruction.

Many of us feel that we have no choice but to protect ourselves from the increasing harshness and horrors of this world by withdrawing, staying busy with minor tasks, suppressing emotions of despair, grief, powerlessness. Some seek comfort by denial, creating personal bubbles to shut the world out. But the desperate effort that goes into withdrawal, suppression, and denial robs us of the very energy we need to be good leaders. The energy now spent on self-protection can be converted into positive energy if we're willing to encounter reality and see it clearly. Facing reality is an empowering act—it can liberate our mind and heart to discern how best to use our power and influence in service for this time.

We cannot change the way the world is, but by opening to the world as it is we may discover that gentleness, decency and bravery are available, not only to us, but to all human beings.

Chögyam Trungpa, Buddhist teacher

What Time Is It
on the Clock of the World?[1]

It is accurate to label this time as uncertain and chaotic, spinning wildly out of control.[2] Every day we experience disruption, swerves in direction, short-term decisions that undo the future, propaganda, slander, lies, blame, denial, violence. Communities and nations are disrupted by terrorist acts, cumbersome bureaucracies block services, people retreat in self-protection and lash out in fear, angry people strike back at their governments, leaders stridently promise security and outcomes that we know can't be true, tensions between people reach hateful proportions, and confusion and exhaustion sink us into despair and cynicism. This is the age of retreat: from one another, from values that held us together, from ideas and practices that encouraged inclusion, from faith in leaders, from belief in basic human goodness.

There are some who define this chaotic time as filled with potential, basing their hopefulness on the workings of chaos described in new science. They want to "blow up" the current system or contribute to its quick demise and use the ensuing chaos as the opportunity to create healthy new systems. Their hope is based on an innocent misunderstanding of the chaos cycle. Chaos can be a generative force for change, or a cause for disintegration and death. Either way, it requires a descent into chaos, when everything falls apart. It is this part of the cycle that we need to prepare for.

The chaos cycle is triggered by changes in the environment; these external changes force the system to abandon its old ways and respond to the new. Everything that held it together—its beliefs, meanings, and structures—no longer work now that the environment has changed. And so the system falls apart. It descends into chaos and finally reaches a bifurcation point, where it has two choices: Either it can reorganize using new beliefs and structures that work well in the changed environment. Or it can insist on the old ways, fail to reorganize itself, and die. Both rebirth and death are possible as an outcome of the passage through chaos.

So there is a slight basis for those who welcome in this time of disruption and chaos as the means to create healthier, more humane and life-affirming ways of living on this planet, for as long as the planet will have us. But we can't get there from here without traversing through the falling apart stage. We cannot simply leap to new ways of being; first we must prepare for disintegration and collapse.

The ceremony of innocence is drowned; The best lack all conviction, while the worst Are full of passionate intensity.

W. B. Yeats, "The Second Coming"

Systems that are failing now will continue to deteriorate. Uncertainty, confusion, and fear will continue to predominate. People will withdraw further into self-protection and strike out at those different from themselves. Corrupt leaders will intensify their false promises, and people will subjugate themselves to their control. The chaos cycle predicts this has to happen, that things must fall apart. And human history documents in astonishingly clear detail the pattern of collapse that all civilizations go through.

———

This book is born of my desire to summon us to be leaders for this time as things fall apart, to reclaim leadership as a noble profession that creates possibility and humaneness in the midst of increasing fear and turmoil.

———

I know it is possible for leaders to use their power and influence, their insight and compassion, to lead people back to an understanding of who we are as human beings, to create the conditions for our basic human qualities of generosity, contribution, community, and love to be evoked no matter what. I know it is possible to experience grace and joy in the midst of tragedy and loss. I know it is possible to create islands of sanity in the midst of wildly disruptive seas. I know it is possible because I have worked with leaders over many years in places that knew chaos and breakdown long before this moment. And I have studied enough history to know that such leaders always arise when they are most needed.

Now it's our turn.

Who Do We Choose to Be?

This needs to be stated clearly at the outset: we can no longer solve the global problems of this time at large-scale levels: poverty, economics, climate change, violence, dehumanization.[3] Even though the solutions have been available for a very long time, they require conditions to implement them that are not available: political courage, collaboration across national boundaries, compassion that supersedes self-interest and greed. These are not only the failings of our specific time in history; they occur in all civilizations at the end of their life cycle.

This is a bitter pill for activists and all people with discerning, open hearts. We understand the complexity of global problems, we have thought systemically to define root causes, we have proposed meaningful solutions, but we are impotent to influence those in power who ignore our efforts.[4]

———

The powerful always defend the status quo because it is the source of their power and privilege. Any change that benefits others would destroy their position. And their position is all they care about defending.

———

As a lifelong activist focused on changing leadership in large systems, as one still inside those large systems as a consultant, advisor, and friend, I realized years ago that large-scale change was not possible. Leaders were grasping for control, overreacting to crises rather than thinking systemically, treating people as "units" rather than as humans. Yet I also met and worked with extraordinary leaders who were creating islands of sanity where good work still got done and where people enjoyed healthy relationships in the midst of chaotic conditions, fierce opposition, heart-breaking defeats, lack of support, isolation, loneliness, and slander. I have been with them in circumstances that caused most other leaders to give up and walk away yet still they kept going. You will learn about a few of them in these pages.

Several years ago, in the face of irreversible global problems and the devolution of leadership, I began to challenge every leader I met with these questions: Who do you choose to be for this time? Are you willing to use whatever power and influence you have to create islands of sanity that evoke and rely on our best human qualities to create, produce, and persevere?

Now I'm asking you.

Two Lenses

Many lenses can be used to bring our current time into focus. Clear seeing is available by studying history, psychology, sociology, anthropology, theology. Each of these disciplines provides concepts and beliefs that explain human behavior both individually and collectively. In this book, I use two lenses: the new science of living systems, and the pattern of collapse in complex civilizations. Each of them is a powerful lens on its own; I have found that together they offer tremendous explanatory power for where we are, how we got here, and the choices we must make as leaders.

Science of Living Systems

The science of living systems is a powerful explanator of human behavior and the world we inhabit. We are alive, we inhabit a living planet, and we are subject to the dynamics of living systems whether we acknowledge them or not. These dynamics are "scale-independent" and can be used to explain what's going on—cause and effect—from single individuals to the entire planet. Why are we witnessing exponential increases in narcissism, polarization, conflict, aggression, dictatorships, climate change, species loss? Each of these terrible realities can be understood using the lens of living systems.

New science revealed, through decades of experimentation and evidence, that living systems organize using dynamics that include self-organizing based on identity, relationships woven together in complex networks, an inherent order displayed in chaos and complexity, the role of shared meaning to create coherent yet nonpoliced actions among individuals.

Globally, a noteworthy minority of leaders in all types of organizations and professions were inspired by these images of creativity and chaos, order without control, interdependent systems growing in capacity and complexity, the primacy of relationships. Such promises motivated many to work to create healthy communities, organizations, and societies. Now, in spite of our years of dedicated efforts, we are greatly fatigued and in deep inquiry as how we might best contribute. And no wonder. Our work, as good and wise as it was, has not born fruit at large levels of scale, even though we have shining examples of what's possible at local levels.[5]

Life's dynamics do not change. They are reliable ways of understanding how life organizes, functions, and responds. This is my intention, to bring a level of understanding to what has happened in the past decades, not so that we can fix the large systems that now dominate and destroy, but so that we can do our work wherever we are, whatever it is, refusing to comply or participate with dominant culture and instead, as leaders, continue to work in partnership with life, restoring sanity wherever we can.

The Pattern of Collapse of Complex Civilizations

As many have commented, the only thing evident from the study of history is that we humans fail to learn from history. Yet those who do study the history of civilizations have illuminated the pattern of the rise and fall of complex human societies. The pattern of collapse is remarkably consistent, describing how humans always behave, even down to specific behaviors. To learn about this pattern is at once very troubling and very relieving: it's good to understand where we are so we don't keep struggling against inevitable behaviors and grievous to see where we are because of what can't be changed. I have delved into the excellent body of literature on the collapse of civilizations for several years now; for this book, I'm primarily working with two: *The Collapse of Complex Societies* by Joseph Tainter and *The Fate of Empires and the Search for Survival* by Sir John Glubb.

Both Glubb and Tainter have derived the pattern of collapse from studying complex human civilizations since Sumer, 3000 BCE. (I have also brought in anthropological research that reveals patterns of behavior going back more than 300,000 years, before hominids were *sapiens*.) Tainter's work, first published in 1987, is acknowledged as the seminal work in establishing the pattern of collapse. He is a superb and dedicated scholar, both humble and clear. Over several years, he studied in depth many different societies; as he did so, the pattern became so clear that he felt no need to continue to study others in detail. "Collapse is a recurrent feature of human societies, and indeed it is this fact that makes it worthwhile to explore a general explanation.... The picture that emerges is of a process recurrent in history and prehistory, and global in its distribution."[6] (See the appendix for Tainter's descriptors of collapse.)

Tainter's analysis of collapse included civilizations on all continents and focuses on the sociopolitical aspects. Sir John Glubb studied thirteen civilizations in Europe, the Middle East, and Asia, observing the process of moral decay from generation to generation that ends in collapse after ten generations. "The life-expectation of a great nation, it appears, commences with a violent, and usually unforeseen, outburst of energy, and ends in a lowering of moral standards, cynicism, pessimism and frivolity."[7] As you will learn here, he describes specific behaviors and attitudes of each age that read like news stories of our current time, but that are characteristic of all civilizations in their final days.

While each scholar highlights different aspects, the pattern is the same: No matter the geography, ethnicity, or spiritual traditions, humans always develop high culture, hierarchy, civic institutions, religion and the arts, and then, when in decline, our negative behaviors are also identical. I feel confident in labeling this the true DNA of our species, how we organize and behave through generations of creation and decline, no matter who we are culturally, where we are geographically, or when we lived in human history.

As I worked with both of these lenses—the science of living systems and the pattern of collapse—I found they were an excellent pair. They could explain how our unique digital culture has intensified our civilization's movement through the last stages of collapse, yet also how the behaviors of each stage are predictable and inevitable.

The reason why complex societies disintegrate is of vital importance to every member of one, and today that includes nearly the entire world population.

Joseph Tainter

The DNA of Human Civilizations: What We Always Create

When the Spaniards reached the American mainland
in the early sixteenth century ... what took place was
truly exceptional, something that had never happened
before and never will again.

Two cultural experiments running in isolation came face
to face and each could recognize the other's institutions.
When Cortes landed in Mexico he found roads, canals, cities,
palaces, schools, law courts, markets, irrigation works, kings,
priests, temples, peasants, artisans, armies, astronomers,
merchants, sports, theater, art, music, and books.

High civilization, differing in the details but alike in essentials,
had evolved independently on both sides of the earth.

Ronald Wright

Form Follows Function: The Design of This Book

For many years, I have needed to know what to do, how best to use my heart and mind and energy to meaningfully serve as things fall apart. This book mirrors my own process: using the lens of new science to understand where we are and how we got here, using the patterns of complex civilizations to deepen my historical awareness and then reflecting on what I've learned from working with leaders who did not lose their way but persevered in doing the best that was possible in difficult, even dire circumstances.

Here is a guide to the design of this book, how I've chosen to organize its many different elements. This is a complex work because it needs to be, and in the next essay I describe "Dwelling Mind" as the way to work with this material slowly and thoughtfully.

I set out to answer three questions, each of which embodies one of the subtitles:

1. *Facing Reality:* Where are we and how did we get here?
2. *Claiming Leadership*: What is the role of leaders now?
3. *Restoring Sanity*: How do we create islands of sanity that sustain our best human qualities?

In every section, these questions are explored in detail in short essays, grouped under these three headings.

I begin each section with *What Science Teaches*—explaining a specific dynamic common to all living systems. I describe how this dynamic is defined and used by scientists to explain observable phenomena in the known Universe. The six dynamics featured are The Arrow of Time; Identity; Information; Self-Organization; Perception; Interconnectedness. (These are very similar to the science I used in *Leadership and the New Science*. This is deliberate.)

Following the science are several essays under the heading *Facing Reality*. In these essays, I use the lens of science to describe the causes of many of our most troubling and disturbing personal and social behaviors, especially those of importance to leaders. These dynamics of living systems work powerfully and irrevocably in us; even if we ignore them, they are always operating. Adding to the lens of science, I use the pattern of collapse of complex civilizations to further understand where we are. Where do our behaviors and cultural phenomena place us on the timeline of collapse?

Here's an example of how these two lenses weave together:

The most powerful organizing dynamic in life is identity. The first act of life is to define a self, whether a micro-organism or a human being. In humans, how we define ourselves determines our perceptions, beliefs, behaviors, values. Today, it is this primary dynamic of identity that drives social media and has led to its overbearing, distorting presence in our lives. Social media enables a culture of manufactured identities, where people create any self that ensures their popularity. In the Digital Age, identity has changed from a culturally transmitted sense of self within a group to an individual one, where you can be anything you want.

In this maelstrom of constantly changing selves, Ideas of objective truth and integrity disappear. Ethics and taking a stand don't matter; popularity does.

This understanding of how identity has created our present-day culture can be easily plotted against Glubb's Six Ages of Collapse. At first, in the Pioneer Age, identities form from a sense of honor and commitment to a cause. Sacrifice and service are the guiding values. Midway, all civilizations evolve into the Age of Commerce, where money and wealth become the organizing identities. Service gives way to getting rich. In the final stage, the Age of Decadence, celebrities—athletes, musicians, and actors—are revered and people lose themselves in wanton pleasures. (In November 2016, President Obama awarded Presidential Medals of Freedom primarily to athletes, musicians, and actors.)

This is one example of how the two lenses combine to sharpen our understanding of where we are, how we got to here, and how best to serve as we journey the well-trodden path of collapse.

Subsequent essays are organized under *Claiming Leadership* and *Restoring Sanity*. In these, I answer the questions, What are we to do as leaders, given this reality? What is sane leadership? I use a combination of commentary, actual practices, quotes, and story to bring into focus the qualities and actions that support good leadership on an island of sanity. The stories I tell are of leaders I worked with closely, who used living systems dynamics in healthy and life-affirming ways. These leaders are exceptionally diverse in who they led (from nuns to military commanders), but deeply unified in how they work with people and partner with life. They are all leaders that people admire for their achievements; I admire them for the depth of their intelligence, integrity, and great hearts and minds. It is an honor to bring them into these pages and into your awareness.

Each of these leaders is a Warrior for the Human Spirit and, in the concluding chapters, I bring in my current work, to train leaders to develop the qualities of compassion, discernment, and presence that are essential leadership skills these days. Starting in the late '90s, I began teaching about spiritual warriorship, how to lead without using aggression or fear to accomplish our goals. I described them in a preliminary way in *So Far from Home* (2012). Since then, I have been actively training leaders globally in the skills of Warriors for the Human Spirit, work that I expect to continue for as long as I am able. Clearly the need for such leaders now grows exponentially.

Dwelling Mind

I have intentionally designed this book for you to read slowly and contemplatively. Curiosity and openness are important generally, but I'm sensitive to the emotional impact of reading this material, absorbing where we are as a civilization. I expect you will be both inspired and overwhelmed, depressed and committed. I had all these experiences as I was writing this. The openness of the pages and the photos are there to encourage you to rest and absorb the material. It's tough to take this in and strong emotions will arise.

I also don't want us to get caught in the ambush of hope. I've read too many authors who lay out the reality of our situation in stark detail, but then in the last pages feel the need to say something hopeful even though it contradicts their own argument. I have no interest in grasping after or reviving possibilities that have already passed. I have an intense desire for us to step forward as leaders for this time, hearts and minds fully open and wise, in service to whomever needs us.

Please don't go through this material quickly. You do a disservice to yourself and to your potential offerings as a leader if you do. I have put in a great deal of information and included many footnotes; I felt these were necessary to develop a depth of understanding. As I was writing, I kept wondering if anybody reads footnotes any more—my publisher tells me that people read the back cover, the front cover, and perhaps the introduction. If you've read this far, it seems you're not that sort of person.

I can't imagine a more important task than to consciously choose who we want to be as a leader for this time. We must understand the time we're in, focus our energy on what's possible, and willingly step forward to serve the human spirit.

This book is designed to invite you into *dwelling mind*.[8] Most of us have the tendency to read something quickly and then rush into action, to quickly figure out a response. As leaders and consultants, this is what we get paid for! It's also a very human approach for dealing with uncertainty and strong emotions—we rush to fix rather than allow the profound discomfort that arises from difficult information. Yet if we dwell with the increasing uncertainty of this time and not rush to that comfortable place of action, dwelling mind supports the emergence of clarity for our chosen role as leaders. This is my frequent personal experience. As I tune into what's going on and allow my grief and outrage to be present, they quietly transform into ever-deepening motivation to offer my best service wherever opportunities present themselves.

I urge you to let go of the comfort of a quick response and instead, in the spaciousness of your mind, welcome in everything: thoughts, feelings, sensations. Allow them to just be there, meeting up with one another, combining and recombining. Nothing is immediately clear, but given time and the workings of nonlinearity, your ideas and feelings may self-organize into insights. Many scientific breakthroughs were the result of this process of relaxing the mind, allowing things to dwell without any need for resolution, and then the a-ha moment. Sometimes scientists were so fatigued or frustrated that they walked away from the problem. They took a stroll or a nap and then were surprised by a clear insight, image, or solution.[9]

If we are to step forward with true confidence as leaders for this time, if this is the role you choose for yourself, then please give your mind and heart time to dwell in the difficulties that lie ahead, and the frequent opportunities we will have to serve the human spirit. In a memorable scene in *Lord of the Rings,* Gandalf counsels Frodo who, in grief and fear, is protesting against his assignment that he must destroy the ring of power, wanting to refuse his destiny.

So do all who live to see such times. But that is not for them to decide. All we have to decide is what to do with the time that is given us.

J. R. R. Tolkien

OPENING: NOTES

[1] This is a question posed by Grace Lee Boggs, the great activist, revolutionary, and community organizer who participated in many of the major social movements in America beginning in the early 1950s. Grace died in Detroit at age 100 in 2015. You'll meet her in Section 4: Self-Organization.

[2] The acronym, coined by the U.S. military, is VUCA—volatile, uncertain, complex, and ambiguous.

[3] See my book *So Far from Home: Lost and Found in Our Brave New World* (Oakland, CA: Berrett-Koehler, 2012).

[4] Pope Francis's encyclical in the spring of 2015, "On Care for Our Common Home" (*Laudato Si*), was a brilliant systemic analysis of causes and solutions to climate change. But these solutions require a level of cooperation between nation-states, dissolution of the huge egos of those in power, and sacrifice from developed nations that will not happen even though the consequences of self-protection rather than intense cooperation are terrifyingly clear.

[5] I'm sure you know of many local efforts that have produced great results. My coauthor Deborah Frieze and I wrote about seven such communities in *Walk Out Walk On: A Learning Journey into Communities Daring to Live the Future Now* (Oakland, CA: Berrett-Koehler, 2011).

[6] Tainter states the objective of his work is to develop a general explanation of collapse, applicable in a variety of contexts, and with implications for current conditions. This is a work of archaeology and history, but more basically of social theory. Joseph A. Tainter, *The Collapse of Complex Societies* (New Studies in Archaeology) (Kindle Location 124).

[7] Sir John Glubb. *The Fate of Empires and Search for Survival* (1976), http://people.uncw.edu/kozloffm/glubb.pdf. Also see the appendix.

[8] The German philosopher Martin Heidegger (1889–1976) introduced the term *dwelling mind* in contrast with *rational mind*.

[9] One of the most well-known examples of this is the story August Kerkulé told of how he discovered the ring shape of the benzene molecule in the 1860s. In a reverie or daydream, he saw a snake seizing its own tail (the ancient symbol of the Ouroboros). This vision, he said, came to him after years of studying the nature of carbon-carbon bonds.

1. THE ARROW OF TIME

—

Everything Has a Beginning,
a Middle, and an End

**Machines wear down and die.
Living systems, if they learn
and adapt, do not.**

What Science Teaches

The observable Universe and everything in it moves in one direction: from birth to death, from hot to cold, from creative energy to useless energy, from order to disorder. Everything comes from what preceded it. Nothing is reversible. This is the Arrow of Time.

The arrow of time applies to all closed systems in the known Universe, but the new sciences revealed that it is not the predetermined fate of living systems. A living system has permeable boundaries and sense-making capacities. It is an open system, capable of exchanging energy with its environment rather than using up a finite amount. If it opens to its environment, it takes in information, a form of energy. It notices changes and disturbances that it then processes, free to choose its response.

This is life's essential process—using cognition and self-organization to adapt and change. A living system can reorganize itself to become more fit, in the evolutionary sense, to survive. Through its exchanges of information, it creates newness and diversity, sustaining itself through shifts, crises, and catastrophes. All of this is possible and commonplace as long as the system remains open, willing to learn and adapt.

However, if a living system closes itself off, there is no possibility for change and growth. Closed systems have no potential for life's adaptive capacity. They work like machines, passive travelers on the arrow of time, deteriorating and losing capacity, predetermined to waste away because of the Second Law of Thermodynamics—the trajectory of heat energy from useful to useless. (The First Law of Thermodynamics states that the *quantity* of energy is always conserved, neither created nor destroyed as it changes form. The Second Law describes how the *quality* of energy deteriorates in a closed system.) In a closed system, every interaction has an energy cost; some amount of its energy becomes useless through its activities. This is entropy, the measure of disordered energy. More entropy describes greater levels of disorder.

What distinguishes living systems from machines is their ability to learn. They resist the arrow of time and the Universe's movement to increasing disorder by using their cognition to adapt. They stay alert to what's going on in their internal and external environments and respond intelligently. A healthy living system is a good learner and can thrive even though its environment is moving toward increasing disorder. But to do so it must be actively engaged and aware.

If living systems close down, they wear down and death is assured.

A civilization is a large, complex society based on the domestication of plants, animals and human beings.
They vary in their makeup but typically have towns, cities, governments, social classes and specialized roles and professions.

Ronald Wright

The Rise and Fall of Civilizations

The movement of civilizations along the arrow of time has been a mesmerizing field of study from the time of classical Greek scholars such as Plato up to our present. Historians want to know what has gone before, not from intellectual curiosity, but from a desire that their current civilization avoid a similar fate. And there is a plethora of examples for study: Globally there have been dozens of complex civilizations during the last 5,000 years of recorded human history (by 3000 BCE there were already seven known to Western scholars). Every one of them illustrates the same pattern of ascendancy and collapse. In addition, excellent archeological research on the causes of decline removes any doubt about the strong commonalities among these civilizations and the descriptive accuracy of the pattern of collapse.

Still, it was astonishing to read of a ninth-century Arab moralist's lament about the celebrity pop singers who flooded the capital city in great numbers singing erotic songs, using obscene language, whose influence on young people degraded their morality and normalized vulgar. Or to read that in the eleventh century, education in the Arab empire changed from learning to technical training for high-paying jobs.

There is nothing new under the sun.

The pattern is crystal-clear. We humans, no matter where we are or what our cultural belief system is, always organize in the same way. We create glorious buildings, cities, transportation and trade routes, music, aqueducts, dance, poetry, theater, sewage systems, canals, pottery, fabrics, farms, statues, monuments. And yet, these magnificent cultural manifestations are guaranteed to disappear, destroyed at the end by disease, famine, or invaders that attack a society already weakened by moral decay and internal warring. We are incredible organizers and creators, and then are brought down by our arrogance, pettiness, and greed. Always.

But in our bright, shiny, techno-optimistic twenty-first-century global culture, we believe we have stepped off the arrow of time. Our technological and scientific genius gives us the capacity to bypass the fate that has overtaken all other complex civilizations. In our arrogance, we believe that we can use our superior intelligence as never before, changing history, bounding forward in great leaps, no longer subject to the arrow of time. We believe we are the height of human evolution rather than just its most recent, predictably problematic manifestation.[1]

The belief in never-ending progress is fueled by our inexplicable arrogance that we can supersede the laws of the Universe. Our constantly expanding technologies and innovations may appear to be adaptive responses to the environment. But this is not true. Quite the opposite: for the first time in history, humans are changing the global environment rather than adapting to it.

—

We are ignoring scientific laws, acting as Masters of the Universe, asserting we can invent anything we want to suit ourselves, including artificial life. This is not the behavior of a living system interacting skillfully with its environment. This is hubris of ahistorical proportions and we are failing miserably, as you may have noted.

For those of us not blinded by the false promise of progress, we may understand the dire state of this civilization. If you're paying any attention to the news from everywhere, it's hard to avoid the specter of collapse. But then what happens? Do we, as most do, fall into private collapse consumed by fear and despair? Do we become one who does nothing but complain for what's been lost? Do we succumb to grief for the suffering of so many? Do we give up and spend whatever time is left in hedonistic pursuits? Do we cocoon in self-protective bubbles with a nine-foot TV screen and SurroundSound?

Or do we acknowledge where we are and step forward to serve? Those who have studied the pattern of collapse always conclude their analyses with an urgent plea that we take notice, that we wake up to where we are in order to positively change where we are. The natural march of time toward disorder can be counteracted and even reversed by awareness and learning. Blind reactivity and fear are not the answer. Self-protection is not the answer. Denial is not the answer. Sane leadership is.

————

What is sane leadership? It is the unshakable faith in people's capacity to be generous, creative and kind.

————

It is the commitment to create the conditions for these capacities to blossom, protected from the external environment. It is the deep knowing that, even in the most dire circumstances, more becomes possible as people engage together with compassion and discernment, self-determining their best way forward.

This leadership is no longer available at the global level. There, the pattern of collapse is manifesting with astonishing speed and accuracy. But within our sphere of influence, there is so much we can do. We can train ourselves to see clearly, to fully acknowledge this time in all its painful details; and then, wherever we are, whoever we're with, we can choose actions based on insight, compassion, and wisdom.

If we choose this role for ourselves, we are joining those few who, throughout history, always step forward to serve in a time of collapse.

While despair might permeate the greater part of the nation, others achieved a new realization of the fact that only readiness for self-sacrifice could enable a community to survive. Some of the greatest saints in history lived in times of national decadence, raising the banner of duty and service against the flood of depravity and despair.

Sir John Glubb

The Decline of Civilizations in Ten Generations

There are many great texts on the pattern of collapse. I chose to feature the work of Sir John Glubb because, in reading his work, I was continually stunned with his descriptions of the specific human behaviors our species always exhibits through the rise and fall of civilizations. I still am likely to gasp as I read his descriptions and share them with others.

Glubb studied thirteen empires in the Middle East, Asia, and Europe (where he had served as a military commander), from Assyria in 859 BCE to modern Britain in 1950. The pattern of the decline and fall of these superpowers was startlingly clear. It didn't matter where they were or what technology they had or how they exercised power. They all declined in the same stages and it always took ten generations, about 250 years. The logic of this is very clear: Each generation matures in better socioeconomic circumstances created by the preceding generation; thus, there is always a march to increasing materialism. In every generation, youth will have higher expectations for comfort than their parents. Improved material conditions create attitudinal changes that insist on still more material changes; and, predictably, because of its wealth and erosion of morality, the civilization declines into decadence.

Here are Glubb's six ages as delineated in *The Fate of Empires*. For more detail, see the appendix. I hope you'll explore them—they are fascinating, troubling, and convincing. As you read these brief descriptions, keep in mind that they describe *all* human civilizations, even though they read like an accurate tale of our time. This was published in 1976.

1. *The Age of Pioneers.* Fearless, courageous, and without constraint, invaders surprise the dominant civilization with their attacks. Strong virtues of shared purpose, honor, and a strict moral code bind them.

2. *The Age of Conquest.* Using more sophisticated and disciplined military actions (learned from the civilization they are conquering), they take control. Often there is a strong religious imperative to their conquest—they are doing their God's work.

3. *The Age of Commerce.* With a strong military to protect the frontiers, explorers embark on a search for wealth creation, seeking new enterprises as far as they can reach. Values of glory and honor give way to values of profit and personal wealth. The rich build palaces, railroads, hotels, communications networks, depending on the cultural context.

4. *The Age of Affluence.* Service ethics disappear and selfishness takes over. Education shifts from learning to obtaining qualifications for high-paying jobs. The young and ambitious seek wealth, not honor or service.

5. *The Age of Intellect.* The arts and knowledge flourish in the midst of decline. Intellectuals are prevalent and engage in incessant talking as a substitute for action. The belief takes hold that problems can be solved by mental cleverness rather than selfless service and courage. Natural sciences advance but do not prevent decline. Civil conflict increases even as the empire is under dire threat. Instead of banding together to preserve the nation, internal political factions seek to destroy one another.

6. *The Age of Decadence.* Wealth and power have led to petty and negative behaviors, including narcissism, consumerism, materialism, nihilism, fanaticism, and high levels of frivolity. A celebrity culture worships athletes, actors, and singers. The masses are distracted by entertainment and sporting events, abandon moral restraint, shirk duties, and insist on entitlements. The leaders believe they are impervious and will govern forever. This age also develops the welfare state as imperial leaders generously build universities and hospitals, give grants to university students, support the young and the poor, and extend citizenship to everyone. When they run out of money, all this benevolence disappears and these institutions shut their doors.

The Myth of Progress

The idea of progress is so ingrained in us high achievers and committed activists that you may be surprised by the word *myth*. Or perhaps you just ignored it. So many of us are motivated to do our best as leaders and good people because we assume that human societies and our species are on an upward evolutionary path, always improving. What would motivate our long hours of dedicated work and our deep longing to create positive change if it isn't true, as Martin Luther King said, quoting others before him: "The arc of the moral universe is long, but it bends toward justice."[2]

Yet the idea of progress is a very recent addition to human thought, appearing in the seventeenth century, reaching full bloom in the nineteenth century, and then severely challenged by the twentieth century's wars that killed more than 100 million people. Progress as a concept or direction does not appear in other cultures, or even in Western thought, until 300 years ago.

It gained ground in the West because of the advent of spectacular machines and great advances in science. It was also supported by Christianity's orientation to an end to time, and a misperception of the theory of evolution that confused evolution with progress.[3] But every other culture has the perspective of cycles throughout time and history: There are good times then bad times. There was a Golden Age and now there is the Dark Age. Humans cannot alter the seasons—or rush past them with optimistic thinking and hard work.

In spite of its anomalous appearance in human history, progress is the water in which we activist, dedicated fish are swimming ever more frantically, gasping for hopeful air. We want to contribute and the nature of that contribution is toward creating a better life, a better world for our children and perhaps even for seven generations, as indigenous people have taught us. Our work is meaningful because it contributes to this arc of history. We depend on being future focused and take pride in this orientation, rightly critical of those who ignore the future —"future eaters," as scientist and historian Tim Flannery named them.[4]

———

The deceit we are engaged in is that we think we are special, that we can transcend history, alter the seasons, and ignore the arrow of time.

———

Surrounded by technology that dazzles us with its capabilities and tech optimists who confidently promise more and more wonders, we have come to believe that even if other civilizations failed, ours will not. It cannot because we are so talented and creative and concerned. Look at all these *amazing* technologies that will soon solve all our problems. Artificial Intelligence (AI); privately funded space travel; artificial foods; farmed fish; pills to make us smart, prevent aging, and prolong sex; medical breakthroughs to grow human organs in animals; neuroscience to fix every problematic behavior—how could anyone deny we're making progress? Some tech leaders are even promising us the prospect of colonizing Mars and beyond. No matter what happens on Earth, we get a second chance. (Well, only a few of us do.)

This belief in technology to fix the messes we've made and to save us from decline has been labeled by Ronald Wright, "The Progress Trap." It appears in every civilization and is a major accelerator of their demise.[5]

The very innovations that gave capacity end up destroying the civilization. People fail to notice or blindly ignore what these technologies are destroying and persist in relying on them until it's too late.

—

This has been true throughout human history. Animal herds were depleted when early humans discovered they could kill thousands of animals by running them off cliffs (one prehistoric site has the remains of over 100,000 horses killed).[6] We continue to pursue industrial production using fossil fuels to give us a higher standard of living, while polluting the air and water that impacts our health and the health of a rapidly heating planet. Artificial fertilizers and seeds were introduced in the Green Revolution to eliminate hunger; as a consequence, we've destroyed soil's regenerative capacities, killed many species, polluted waterways, and caused hundreds of thousands of farmers to commit suicide. And now, who knows what we're destroying with the ecstatic rush to automation, including self-driving cars, robots, AI in everything, and package delivery by drones.

Technology doesn't save us. It promises a Utopian future, but, in the record of history, it eventually destroys with its unintended consequences. This is the true arc of history, not upward toward some halcyon future but as dissipative movement along the arrow of time. We believe we can push aside input from the environment and, with intense creativity and innovation, soar off the arrow of time. Meanwhile, the environment we've refused to interact with continues its relentless march to greater disorder.

But isn't all this fabulous, *amazing* growth in new technologies an example of the fiery creative energy at the start of a new civilization? Aren't we as innovators and entrepreneurs starting a new world that counteracts the forces of entropy? Aren't we in the Golden Age, Masters of the Universe, setting a new direction toward evolutionary progress and bright futures?

No.

Lost in the seduction of technical creativity, we fail to see what else is going on. What's happening in society to relationships, to poverty, to violence, to alienation? What's happening to our land, our traditions, our people? Why have more than 65 million people fled their home countries and now live as refugees? What's being done to address our enduring human needs for home, for community, for contribution, for good work, for safe children?

And what about our planet?

Wise leaders are willing to give up the delusion that technology can save us, or that we can master the Universe. We must face the reality of decline and choose actions that support people, not technology. The choice couldn't be more clear. Or consequential.

Digital technologies, rather than inviting us into the world

and encouraging us to develop new talents that enlarge our

perceptions and expand our possibilities,

often have the opposite effect.

They're designed to be disinviting.

They pull us away from the world....

The computer screen is intensely compelling,

not only for the conveniences it offers

but also for the many diversions it provides....

Yet the screen, for all its enticements and stimulations,

is an environment of sparseness—

fast-moving, efficient, clean,

but revealing only a shadow of the world.

Nicholas Carr, The Glass Cage

The Religion of "Technological Majesty"

1833   By fulfilling its mechanical purposes, the US would turn itself into a new Eden, a state of superabundance where there will be a continual feast, parties of pleasures, novelties, delights and instructive occupations, not to mention vegetables of infinite variety and appearance.

      — *John Adolphus Etzler*,

          The Paradise Within the Reach of All Men (1833)

1991   What better way to emulate God's knowledge than to generate a virtual world constituted by bits of information?

      — *Michael Heim*, philosopher

2005   Behold, we are entering a new world, powered not by God's grace but by the web's electricity of participation. It will be a paradise of our own making, manufactured by users. History's databases will be erased, humankind rebooted. You and I are alive at this moment.

      — *Wired*, August 2005 cover article on Web 2.0

2014 For the first time in history, humankind, liberated by computers and robots from physical constraints, will be able to express its full and true nature. We will be whoever we want to be.... The main fields of human endeavor will be culture, arts, sciences, creativity, philosophy, experimentation, exploration, adventure.

— *Marc Andreessen*, venture capitalist

2016 Elon Musk, CEO of SpaceX and Tesla, speaking at an event for tech industry leaders, offers a mind-blowing future of neural lace implanted in the human jugular, a representative democracy on Mars, and the real possibility that we're living in a video game simulation.

— All quotes in Carr, *Utopia Is Scary* except Elon Musk speaking at CODE, June 2, 2016

Tipping Points

Our bias toward progress is easily seen in how we view "tipping points," a bona fide scientific principle in physics, now adopted by social change activists. The original term means turning points or phase transitions, the last straw that breaks the camel's back when the system suddenly shifts into a new state. Yet in popular lingo, the concept has been adopted as the way to create positive social change in the future. People I know have been working to create a percentage of people so that the scales will tip and suddenly we'll find ourselves in a bright new future. How many people does it take to create the tip? Estimates have varied widely but start with speculation that as few as 10 percent of a population can create the sudden shift. Yet none of these estimates have been validated in experience.

The existence of tipping points is beyond dispute; at a certain point, criticality is reached and the system changes rapidly into a new state. But rather than remaining blindly optimistic about the statistical chances of positive future change, let's notice what's already tipped, those points of no return already passed, where the task now is to deal with the frightening consequences. What tipping points have already occurred?

- CO_2 emissions, parts per million above 400
- Warming oceans—Great Barrier Reef bleaching, ice-free Arctic
- Glaciers melting far faster than projected
- Rising sea levels—threat of melting Greenland ice sheet
- Atmospheric temperatures climbing steadily
- Clean water
- Population
- Sixth global mass extinction
- People's anger and frustration

Choosing to Lead Well in Collapse

What does it mean to be a leader in a time of collapse?

While there are very destructive dynamics at play as our civilization travels down the arrow of time, these dynamics do not have to wield influence on anyone or any group that is willing to open to its environment, use its intelligence, and bravely face reality. Whenever we open rather than close we become alive, a living system capable of self-organizing into new order rather than succumbing to disorder. The good news is that this is happening in many places, enlivened places resisting disorder by using their hearts and minds well. And every one of them is grounded in an ethic that places people at the center of all decisions and actions. Sanity in action.

In the tragedies of the refugee crisis, in the complexities of a broken healthcare system, in communities torn apart by fear and hatred, in exhausted professionals who find a new way to serve—everywhere there are communities, programs, and organizations that are learning, adapting, and creating effective responses that are making a true and positive contribution. But we need to keep this in perspective.

—

These leaders cannot prevent the unraveling of our global civilization and that is not their ambition. They aspire to make a profound difference locally, in the lives of people in their communities and organizations.

They also know that their successful initiatives that took such dedication and endurance to create are vulnerable to the destructive politics and behaviors inherent in a dying culture. At any moment, they or their programs may be swept away or severely hampered by thoughtless or venal political decisions. There are no assurances they will achieve long-term impact or be rewarded for success from the leaders above them who are possessed by fear and panic.

And yet they persevere because they are committed to doing the best they can for people. They have learned that nearly all people desire to do good work in good relationships with their colleagues. In full awareness of the trials and tribulations that will not cease, they offer their leadership skills to create islands of sanity, places of possibility and sanctuary where the destructive dynamics of collapse are kept at bay.

For as long as they can.

We do good work because we do good work.

Angela Blanchard, CEO

Dancing in the Space of Sanity

Chögyam Trungpa had the ability to draw forth

from those he worked with the very best they had to offer—

sometimes better than they had to offer.

He gave them a glimpse of just how glorious they could be.

Then, he left it up to all of us to work out

how to actually become those great human beings

we keep buried inside us most of the time.

He created a space of absolute sanity in which we all danced.

Carolyn Gimian[7]

Leading an Island of Sanity

What does it take to lead an island of sanity? What does the practice of sane leadership look like? Is it possible to create protection from the wild irrationality raging about us?

This is where it gets simple.

Even though there is now a vast body of work on leadership, I find it far more enlightening to consult our personal histories. All of us have had multiple experiences with good and bad leaders, from kids working in fast-food franchises to retirees with more than forty years of work history. When asked (which I've done thousands of times), "What is good leadership?" people in all places, of all ages, come up with the same descriptors. I feel confident that there is only one style, type, form of leadership that people respond well to. And they respond because it honors and supports them to be fully human. Just like we respond.

To determine your own definition of good leadership, think about your history:

1. Recall those leaders you've most admired, those you were happy to serve under. What were their behaviors? How did you feel working for them? What kind of worker were you, including the quality of what you produced? How do you feel about them now?
2. Recall your own moments when you were proud of the leadership (either formal or informal) you provided to your organization, family, friends, community. What did you do? How did you behave toward others? What were the results of your leadership? Are you still in a relationship with any of these people?

Answer these questions and you'll know how to be a good leader on your island. (Please don't bring in images of reality TV shows when I use this term.) And if you're frustrated that I haven't specified the traits of good leaders that I find common among all human beings, may I refer you to my other books?

I'm approaching this lightheartedly because a core survival skill in difficult situations is to maintain a sense of humor. Even with the intensity of feelings that flood over us as we contemplate collapse, it's essential that we not take everything so seriously.

———

The Hopi prophecy for these times teaches, "At this time in history we are to take nothing personally, least of all ourselves, for the moment we do, our spiritual growth and journey comes to a halt."[8]

———

Yes, these are terrifying times if we open our eyes. Yes, our heart aches for all the needless suffering and destruction. And yes, maintaining a sense of humor gives us the capacity to observe the suffering and failures with enough distance that we can see it all more clearly. Irony and humor (not sarcasm) are critical skills to wise discernment. In order to laugh, we have to take in a lot of information and see things from a different perspective. Sarcasm, on the other hand, is just observing from a distance through the eyes of cynicism. It does not connect us in any way. It does not enable action or relationship. And it is growing exponentially in this culture. Even my very young grandchildren are skilled at sarcasm.

I should like to think that prehistoric man's first invention, the first condition for his survival, was a sense of humor.

Andre Leroi-Gourhan, paleoanthropologist

Where Is Your Organization on the Arrow of Time?

It is easy, although painful, to observe the decay and degradation of the human spirit and of our planet at the global, national, and local levels. But what's going on in our own organizations? How can we assess our health versus our decay? As we attempt to fortify ourselves with sanity rather than fear, to open rather than close, what requires our attention?

Here are some of the characteristics of systems in decline. In all the descriptions of the pattern of collapse, there is both the human element of moral decay and the systemic element of institutional rot. Increasing disorder is fueled by money replacing service as the core motivator, hierarchical leaders focused on maintaining power at all costs, the disappearance of the future from decision making, the preservation of the status quo by the few elites who prosper from it. As things deteriorate, relationships disintegrate into distrust, self-protection, and opposition. Internal conflicts increase and no one even notices threats to the whole as they fight for their tiny piece of the pie. Leaders use fear to control and manipulate people and everyone moves into self-protection. Distractions, entertainments, and entitlements become primary instruments of allaying people's fears and for controlling them.

Translating these predictable behaviors into assessments of an organization seems quite straightforward. Please develop your own; here are some that have proven useful in my work. It's more helpful to answer these in terms of trends rather than snapshots. The real learning comes from noticing what's changing, and in which direction, as you explore each topic.

Each of these explorations demonstrates your commitment to opening to what is. This in itself is important. It gives you a start to interrupting the destructive trends of our culture and offers possibilities for engaging people to join you in developing an island of sanity.

—

Quality of relationships: If you were to create a trend line from a few years ago to now and a few years ahead, how are people relating to each other? Has trust increased or declined? Are people more self-protective or less so? Are they more willing to be there for one another, to go the extra mile, or not? What's your evidence for any of your conclusions?

Fear versus love: If these are the two ends of the spectrum of human emotions, which I believe they are, consider where you see examples of each. Also look for tendencies: which reaction, fear or love, is more likely in specific situations or with specific issues? Are either of these emotions coming to dominate as time goes on? In your leadership, what role does fear play: Are you more fearful? Are you using fear to motivate people?

Quality of thinking: When a crisis happens, how do you respond? Are your values used to resolve the crisis? Do you consider the future? Is long-term thinking still happening (in conversations, decision making, planning)? Has it made an impact? If so, is this visible to people? How difficult is it to find time to think, both for yourself and others?

Willingness to contribute: What invitations to contribute have you extended and why? How have people responded? Ongoing, what are your expectations for people being willing to step forward? Are those higher or lower than a few years ago?

The role of money: How big an influence, as a percentage of other criteria, do financial issues have on decisions? Has money become a motivator for you? For staff? Has selfishness replaced service? How do you know?

Other indicators, especially around learning from experience, are described in later chapters. For now, any of these topics answered with curiosity and concern can yield enormous benefit to your aspiration to be a good leader for this time. And they are questions that yield critical information for any attempt to bring greater sanity into the organization and among us as colleagues.

Leading from the Future

In 1993, I was invited by the Army Chief of Staff, General Gordon R. Sullivan, to be his "scout." The Army, under his leadership, was focused on bringing the force out of its worst period of decline, the Vietnam War era, and preparing it for the twenty-first century. For the next two years, and many times thereafter, I got to know the military. It was where I learned about dedication, service, and warriorship. It was my introduction to a rare form of leadership, vigilantly focused on the future, rapidly absorbing and making sense of information, with no room for failure.

General Sullivan remains one of the most extraordinary leaders I've known. When he asked me to be his scout, at first I thought this was a cute metaphor, the kind we consultants might use. I quickly realized this was a specific role, familiar in the military, to be taken very seriously. I was sent out to many places where innovations were taking place, met with all ranks of soldiers, and generally became familiar with the Army's change initiatives. Then I reported back to General Sullivan and we delved deeply into what I had seen and the potential meaning of my observations.

To this day, my respect for soldiers has never waivered. Their leadership training is far superior to anything I've encountered elsewhere: They are taught how to process large amounts of information, to think systemically, to develop situational awareness, to lead in chaotic situations, to lead from behind as well as out front, to use their intuition. And everything depends on teamwork. Soldiers know their lives depend on being there for each other. I've relished every chance I've had to teach military officers. Their intelligence, curiosity, and esprit de corps are palpable; it's easy to engage them in vibrant and complex learning.

General Sullivan had invited me because of my work with self-organization and the role of information. In working with the Army, I learned more than I could have imagined about the power of self-organization to bring order out of chaos. At the time I came in, soldiers had just been armed with new technologies that gave them real-time information about the battle. Once they could see what was going on, they demanded to be involved in decisions. Unlike most organizations, the Army quickly realized that, with such information, soldiers could self-organize their responses and make better decisions in the chaos of battle than any command and control system. Later, in Iraq, the quick exchange of electronic information from soldier to soldier saved lives—moment by moment they could relay where the explosives were hidden, what new traps to watch out for. A now-famous self-organized community of practice emerged among captains, Company Command.[9] They became adept at rapidly communicating tactics and strategies faster than the established protocol of Army Lessons Learned. Company Command is credited with saving thousands of lives.

———

Senior commanders learned that well-trained soldiers could be trusted to process information in real time; the soldiers would make better decisions about the battle than if they had to wait for a command from above. Rapidly exchanged information became the critical factor, rather than rank or procedures, to reduce the chaos of conflict.

———

General Sullivan once told me that he spent 50 percent of his time focused on the future. In one conversation I will never forget, he said, "Sometimes I get afraid. What if there's another war and we're not prepared?" In that moment, I had a brief, frightening glimpse of what it means to carry the defense of the free world on your shoulders. We had just been in an inquiry, which included the Army historian and a few four-star generals, as to whether the Army should keep investing in tank training. What would warfare look like over the next decades? (This was in 1994; by 2005, the Army had prioritized resources for Special Operations, small cadres of brilliantly trained soldiers to operate in war zones and undercover against insurgent groups.)

When he voiced his deepest concern about being prepared for an unknown future, our inquiry about future battlefields became deadly serious. Perhaps the generals had been viewing it that way all along, but for me it was a dramatic wake-up call to be in this deliberation with the greatest intelligence and insight I could muster. It stands out for me as memorable because of the thousands of conversations I've been in with leaders since then that lacked this sense of consequence.

I believe that General Sullivan was unique in focusing 50 percent of his time and efforts on the future. Sometimes he spoke about the challenge of not getting too far ahead of the troops, of having to bring them along—and how difficult that was. The more clearly he saw the imperatives of the future, the greater his frustration with the ponderously slow movement of the Army so laden down with tradition and bureaucracy.

How many leaders spend time in the future? How many decisions are made using information from both present realities and future scenarios? How many organizations are willing to open their boundaries and absorb as much information as they can, knowing that it is only these exchanges that prevent deterioration and death?

How many leaders understand how to step off the arrow of time and consciously engage with the future so as to influence its direction, not with complex strategies but by using information well? General Sullivan's leadership was rare then. Now it is an endangered species.

—

The last time I was with General Sullivan was at a scenario planning session hosted by Shell Oil Company at Windows on the World atop the World Trade Center, just a few years before the attacks of 9/11. He voiced his frustration to me about the behavior he was encountering on the corporate boards where he now served. "We spend hours debating how to get the stock price up a penny. Nobody is thinking about development of leaders or the future."

THE ARROW OF TIME: NOTES

[1] For a brilliant brief history of how our economics is tied to the belief in progress, read Pankaj Mishra, "Welcome to the Age of Anger," theguardian.com, December 18, 2016. https://www.theguardian.com/politics/2016/dec/08/welcome-age-anger-brexit-trump

[2] I've been puzzled by this assertion of the arc of justice growing stronger over long periods of time because it cannot be verified historically. But within the last stage of collapse, the Age of Decadence, human rights, social justice, gender equality, education, and healthcare benefits all surge ahead as leaders create the welfare state. The leaders, acting as if they'll always be in power with unlimited resources, are hugely beneficent in offering a progressive society to all. So it appears that justice and the social good are moving forward, which they are in the context of the moment and the past few years of the civilization. However, the tragic irony is that all this progress in human rights occurs at the end of the civilization and cannot be sustained because of all the other forces at play. The arc of justice seems to surge, but it is actually a sign of imminent collapse. Such a harsh truth to contemplate.

[3] Evolution has become a synonym for progress, but this is not the science. Evolution describes adaptations that make the organism more fit for its current environment. That environment can be improving or deteriorating. The survival of any species depends on its recognition of how the environment has changed and what it demands if the species is to survive. Adaptations are not necessarily improvements or progress; they are intelligent responses to what has changed.

[4] Tim Flannery, *The Future Eaters: An Ecological History of the Australasian Lands and People* (Grove Press, 1994).

[5] *A Short History of Progress*.

[6] Ibid., p. 50.

[7] *True Command: The Teachings of the Dorje Kasung* Vol I, "The Town Talks," ed. Chögyam Trungpa and Carolyn Gimian (Halifax: Trident, 2005; out of print).

[8] See my book *Perseverance* (2010), a day-to-day guide that draws on this Hopi prophecy.

[9] *Company Command: Unleashing the Power of the Army Profession* (West Point, NY: U.S. Military Academy, 2005) tells the history of this powerful community of practice, written by its founders.

2. IDENTITY

Living Systems Change in Order
to Preserve Themselves

The first act of life
is to create a boundary,
a membrane that is
the cell's identity.
It defines an inside and
an outside, what it is,
what it is not.

— Margaret Wheatley

What Science Teaches

Living systems create themselves. They (we) are all self-authoring. We always and only organize around an identity, a membrane or boundary that distinguishes us from everything else. Without identity, there would be no means to differentiate one thing from another. There would be no possibility to organize into greater complexity and order. Without identity, it would be a never-ending mess of primordial soup devoid of form and possibility.

There are alternate theories for how life began about four billion years ago, how the first chemical reactions occurred to create the first cells. Where did the energy for those first chemical reactions come from? Was it in the primordial soup of ocean struck by lightning, or in heat vents deep on the ocean floor, or on the new planet's fiery surface? What we do know is that life began with membranes, with boundaries that created cells by separating them from everything else.

Inside that container, possibilities arise—complex interactions that create different and sophisticated functions.[1] The membrane is semipermeable, letting in energy and matter in continual exchanges with its environment. Without that permeability, nothing new could be created, and, like all closed systems, the young life form would quickly wear down and die.

Life cannot be sustained when the boundary becomes rigid. Nor can it generate new capacities and adapt to its environment if the boundary is too open. Too much permeability is as dangerous to the continuation of a living system as is too much rigidity. Maintaining the sensitive balance between open and closed is the ever-present challenge for a living system.

Whenever a living system changes, it is attempting to save itself, to preserve its identity. Every living being has the freedom to use cognition to notice changes in its environment, interpret them, and decide how to respond. Nothing is predetermined—if a change happens, it is the result of the organism's decision to change based on a perceived threat to itself. This is the intriguing paradox of identity: it can be greatly changed as the means to protect its existing self.

———

Without identity there is no life, no creation, no responsiveness, no continuation, no possibility for evolutionary change. Yet every change is motivated by an attempt to preserve a self.

———

You can prove this to yourself. Whenever you detect a change in a person, community, organization, or nation, observe how their old identity is referred to, sometimes many times over, even though they now appear quite changed. (You can also try this at home.) You will always find identity as the reference for change. It cannot be otherwise.

Identity Then and Now

The importance of identity as an organizing dynamic for people and all living beings cannot be overemphasized. It always has and forever will be the basis for how we define ourselves as individuals and societies, the choices we make, the things we attend to, the behaviors we manifest. So it's important to look at how identity has functioned over time into our present day.

Traditionally, cultures defined identity. Who you were, what you thought, what you did were predetermined by where you were born. Identity was never a personal choice. The community raised you with a clear moral sense of right and wrong and gave you a set of beliefs, expectations, and ways of living that bound you to the group with a strong sense of belonging. At some point you may have rebelled, left the community, and sought your freedom to express yourself. But when it came time to raise your children, chances are you were drawn back to your culture whose value now seemed obvious.

Cultural identity can continue for centuries, even millennia, providing ground and continuity. But as is happening now, wars and famine force people to relocate. This has been going on since the beginning of human history, but the scale of this in modern times is one of the most challenging problems for the nations of the affluent world. And one they are retreating from in self-protection. There are more than 65 million refugees; even if wars miraculously were to cease, their numbers will keep growing because of climate change.[2]

Global Culture

In Minneapolis airport
the Somalis serve us
hungry weary travelers with
innocent true smiles

when they began
their long march westward
fleeing violence
terrors on their path
hunger in their bones
only hope and fear
to prod them on

did they ever dream
of this day when
they would smile again
as they serve me a latte
tall dark skinny.

Margaret Wheatley

Most indigenous cultures, their traditions and languages, are being lost to the pressures of global culture at rates even greater than that for the extinction of biological species.[3]

———

People who are dislocated from their homelands and their traditions experience profound loss and disorientation. Their pain is far more than physical; it is also deeply emotional and spiritual as they are uprooted from all that has anchored them.

Global culture has taken hold, a new reality easy to identify in the things we share at the consumer level in music, movies, fashion, food, products, technology. And at the personal level in alienation, addiction, violence, and suicide. The premise of this culture is personal freedom, the right to create yourself in any way you want, unhampered by the past, free to fly without any need for ground. If you are born in the right place, you are free to dream, to follow your passion, to redefine yourself whenever and however you choose. If you are born anywhere else, you watch this display of freedom with envy and resentment that can erupt in fury. Those who fly free in self-absorption fail to see those taking aim at them from below.

A culture focused on individual freedom can only result in narcissism, polarization, conflict, estrangement, and loneliness. What is the meaning of life when it's all about me?

———

In the Age of Decadence that Glubb describes, everyone is focused on their self-interest. Elites protect their wealth, leaders protect their power, and the masses clamor for entertainment. We worship actors, musicians, and athletes. We are bought off with food and grand spectacles; we become obsessed with sports. And we grow more and more demanding; we feel entitled not because we've earned it, but just because we can demand it. And leaders respond because they want to keep us quiet.

I know this sounds depressingly familiar, so let me remind you that this is how humans always behave during the decline of their civilization. Always.

But let me get more precise (and depressing) in describing the particular forces in our civilization that are driving us deeper into the dark morass of individual identity. Understanding these forces also offers us clarity as leaders about how to avoid this descent as we endeavor to create islands of sanity. So do not despair—this analysis can prove beneficial because we need to know how to work well with this primary organizing dynamic of identity. (Was that a spoiler alert?)

In global culture, identity not only is self-created—it is manufactured to be self-promoting. Popularity now is the measure of success personally and politically. It's not what you stand for, but whether your most recent persona creates followers, fans, and votes. The tools for identity manufacture are right at our fingertips, in social media, where we can build our image by posting pictures, videos, blogs, links, comments. Instantly we know what others think about us, what they liked or disliked. Online we can find those with seemingly identical beliefs and together certify that our beliefs and prejudices are the truth. As online consumers, marketeers know us all too well through algorithms that identify and predict our buying preferences; those preferences are then manipulated into purchases to satisfy needs we didn't know we had (because we didn't).[4]

This maelstrom of fake and manipulated identities is only possible because we seem unable to find any other basis for self-identification. Exhausted by the consumption and entertainment, or because of it, we grow talented at sarcasm. Cynicism takes over and with it the descent into meaninglessness. We don't know who we are or why anything is important.

——

We could have been anything we wanted, yet our free-floating individualism has taken us far from community, contribution or connection, the very things that truly give life meaning and purpose.

The Rise of Celebrity Culture

A celebrity culture always arises in the Age of Decadence. We become obsessed with the lives of particular individuals, their talents and achievements. We may find them brilliant or despicable. Whether we are inspired, jealous, critical, or turned off, the focus is on individuals, what they are doing moment by moment and whether they please us. Popularity becomes the measure of success. These distractions grow ever more enticing as things worsen.

———

Cultures focused on popularity have no depth or resilience. They are superficial and ephemeral: tastes change; fashions come and go; fads rise and fall. Always changing, such a culture increases our sense of uncertainty and vulnerability. We may be popular now, but beneath the surface our anxiety and stress keep growing. Will you still love me tomorrow?

———

Think about how technology has exacerbated celebrity culture and raised popularity to the equivalent of the meaning of life. Social media and online selling have pushed popularity to new heights, using it to motivate our behavior—buy this because it's a trend; buy this because your friends have; check out how many "likes" you got on your last post or photo; like this restaurant or website and earn a prize. I won't go on—it's pervasive everywhere online. But here's a headline from my local paper that caught my attention: "Utah County Jail Receives High Rating, Positive Feedback on Google Reviews."

Noting how our technology has enabled the cult of popularity is a good example of the progress trap. Online communications appeared to be wonderful progress—we could exchange photos, shop with ease, stay connected to family, get instant answers to questions, talk to people anywhere on the planet. But now it's obvious how online capacities have, as unintended consequences, morphed into destructive cultural impacts. Narcissism has intensified; hate and "haters" now plague social media, public rallies, and communities; addictive online behaviors waste both time and lives; social skills deteriorate in those living online; patience is obsolete; reflective thinking is antiquated; boredom no longer exists; distractions proliferate and endanger. (Another headline from the *New York Times*: "General: Marines, Put Down Those Cell Phones!")

Communication on social media moves in one direction, toward increased emotionality and distortion of message. If you engage in rapid message exchanges via Facebook or texting, notice what happens to the "conversation" as you go back and forth. The speed of response predicts that communications will become more intense: emotions will rise, miscommunication develop. If things become uncomfortable, people either disappear or offer a superficial ending, usually a series of emojis. How often do such exchanges move into real conversations?

We may be in contact, but we're not connecting. We whiz by each other at cyberspace speed. No dwelling mind here! The Internet rewards speed over all else, and some of the statistics about our craving for speed are mind-boggling. In 2006, Forrester Research found that online shoppers expected web pages to load in under four seconds. Three years later in 2009, the number was shaved to two seconds; slower web pages led many shoppers to look elsewhere. By 2012, Google engineers had discovered that when results take longer than two-fifths of a second to appear, people search less, and *lagging just one-quarter of a second* behind a rival site can drive users away.[5]

Because of all the good things the Internet gave us, until recently we failed to notice that we're entrapped. It's not a question of a cost/benefit analysis, although many people are still stuck there, wanting to acknowledge and hold onto all the benefits to our lives brought by social media even as we face its destructive impacts.

It doesn't balance out. We have to recognize that this wondrous technology has distorted and corrupted the capacities and needs that human beings require to live: intimacy, thinking, listening, meaning making, being present. We need to come face-to-face with the destruction that social media has reaped to our ability to live well together.

More speed, new apps, artificial intelligence, more connectivity through technology is not the answer. Sane leadership is.

The Compelling Call of Identity

We humans use identity to organize our actions and beliefs to give meaning to our lives. We, like all living beings, live in networks of relationship. And like all living beings, we need to stay alert to what's going on in our environment, what might require us to adapt and change.

Amid all the information available in our environment, which identity filter(s) do you use? Are you dedicated to popularity, to a role, to a cause, an ethic, a nation, an ethnicity? What identity gives meaning to your life?

While celebrity culture offers an escape from reality, there are two potent examples today of how identity can be a compelling dynamic for sacrifice and service. This dynamic appears in the early stages of a new civilization when invaders band together to subvert and conquer a decadent culture. Today we see this in the rise of terrorist groups around the world. And it is also true of those who, living inside the decadence of this culture, are willing to sacrifice and work to restore moral virtues such as justice, equality, and compassion. Today we call this form of activism "identity politics."[6]

In putting these two examples of social activists and terrorists in the same paragraph, please note that I am *not* saying they are at all similar in their intentions or methods. What they illustrate, in very different ways, is the power of identity to mobilize people into purposeful actions, foregoing self-promotion and self-protection. As leaders, it is important for us to take note of the incredible power of identity.

Even knowing the power of this dynamic, I keep asking how is it possible for terrorists to lose all sense of personal identity, strap a suicide belt on themselves, spend weeks building bombs to kill and maim, and then go kill themselves?

___

How is it possible for a person to kill colleagues at an office Christmas party? How is it possible to deliberately target children or to be a child who commits these actions?

___

There is so much to understand in these continuing horrific examples, but at their core is an individual or a group that has been influenced to believe that what gives meaning to their lives is killing themselves and murdering people on behalf of a cause. (It is the premeditated suicide that distinguishes their behavior from soldiers who go to war. Soldiers are willing to sacrifice their lives for their nation or cause, and they may kill many people in military operations, but they want to return home alive.)

We know that these young men and women feel hopeless about their own future, that they feel excluded and invisible, that a few of them are mentally ill.[7] We know that drugs, brainwashing, and the availability of thousands of online videos turn them into suicide bombers. Suicide is on the rise globally, especially among youth.[8] These young people have been conditioned to eagerly accept an ideology that gives meaning to their desire to die and erase the pain of life.

The very function of identity—to respond and change in order to survive—has been inverted. It is hard to identify with this upside-down world. No wonder we can't understand it.

——

What is much easier to understand is the rise of identity politics, people organizing on the basis of their marginalization from the rest of society. They unite in their demands for fair treatment, justice, equal rights, access. It can be race, gender, sexual identity, ethnicity, nationality, age—any of the "isms" that flood public discourse these days. They stand in solidarity and gain visibility through many forms of protest. This is happening in many different countries on all continents. Because of their experiences of oppression, neglect, violence, they demand their country pay attention to the values, laws, and practices that, at an earlier time, were recognized as important to that national identity or were pledged in UN resolutions. In the United States, we may never have achieved the goals we set for ourselves as a nation, but they were important enough to struggle for in many wars and social movements.

If you're not at the table, you're probably on the menu.

Elizabeth Warren, U.S. Senator

These values and practices constituted our national identity before we became so distressingly decadent. Is it possible to reclaim them? Are we even interested?

There is an unavoidable consequence when people from the margins organize.[9] The burden of change and the restoration of national values get placed on them. If you want equal rights, it's your job to fight for them. If you demand equal pay, convince us. If you want to be included at the table, prove yourself. The very values that defined who we wanted to be as a nation are no longer defended by the nation. Instead, those who are marginalized must speak loud enough to get our attention. It's no wonder that they end up screaming. And when they finally do get our attention, more often than not we blame them for raising the issue. Either we're doing fine, or it's their fault that we failed. Anger intensifies on both sides, polarization increases, and any ideal of national identity is trampled beyond recognition.

Such civil divisions are predictable in a declining civilization. Instead of uniting in common cause to protect the nation from real threats, we take ourselves down by ever more hateful exchanges.

We are not protecting.
We are protecting.

Native Water Protectors at Standing Rock, 2016

Whatever Happened to Ethics?

We can't avoid noticing the increase in lying, cover-ups, fake apologies, and a growing distrust of leaders in general. One of the more disturbing phenomena is how public figures make a statement that is recorded on video, then several months later say the direct opposite while denying there's any contradiction, if they even notice. When it's pointed out to them, they insist that either they never said the earlier statement or that there's no conflict between the two. It's our problem if we think there's a problem. Probably we're biased against them, or the system is rigged. This is easy fodder for comedians, but very troubling to those who remember other times when what you said publicly meant something because you said it publicly.

We now live in the "post-truth era." *Oxford Dictionary* selected "post-truth" as 2016's international word of the year, based on contentious elections in America and the U.K.

———

Post-truth is defined as "relating to or denoting circumstances in which objective facts are less influential in shaping public opinion than appeals to emotion and personal belief."[10]

———

Instead of coining a new word, what about those good old-fashioned words like *lying, deceit, manipulation*?

Also troubling is the frequent experience of leaders avoiding or denying there's an issue, refusing to take action and then issuing moralistic statements about the issue that are designed to take pressure off of them while simultaneously inspiring us. And if anyone has made progress on the issue, leaders who were critics step forward to take all the credit.

Contradictions and falsehoods don't matter anymore. Neither does evidence. When we try to hold people accountable for their inconsistencies and lies, they just brush us off.

How has this become possible?

It has become possible in the Age of Manufactured Identities because the only thing that is important is your approval rating at this present moment. Of course it's fine to change positions if it gets you what you want. Of course you need to stay abreast of public opinion and respond to its shifts. Of course you can deny the existence of earlier statements when you said contradictory things because that persona is no longer relevant to the current scene. Of course it doesn't matter what you said then because the smart politician gives people what they need to hear from their leader now.

A system of morality which is based on relative emotional values is a mere illusion, a thoroughly vulgar conception which has nothing sound in it and nothing true.

Socrates, Phaedo

It is so easy to refute reality when society sanctions identity creation as a finely honed skill and admires its shifting nature. Make up whatever is most convenient in the moment and do it well so your ratings improve. Blast it out on social media so that people will love you. If it lands, be more of that. If it fails to win approval, make up something else.

Ethics are rules for how to live together. Moral principles mediate our interactions by establishing expectations of how to behave. All spiritual traditions have a clear code of ethics so that people can grow and prosper *as* a community, restrain individual impulses, and together withstand challenges great and small. This is always the role of ethics, to bind together individuals in trustworthy relationships so we can stay together through the vicissitudes of life.

———

Ethics are how we behave when we decide we belong together.[11]

———

Ethics are designed to serve us in community; they have no relevance to individuals who live in isolation or self-absorption, where there is no concern for others. Without ethics, there is no social coherence, no community resilience. Without ethics, it becomes a dog-eat-dog world. Such as many of us are now experiencing in this popularity culture.

Worrying about how others see you is very different from worrying about how others are doing. Self-focused individualism and ethics are direct opposites. And without ethical standards, what is the meaning of personal integrity?

Communities with a strong code of ethics can make decisions, judge actions, and hold one another accountable. Violations and code breaking are easy to identify. Punishments, even when barbaric in our eyes, are accepted because they are predefined by the code. In organizations, shared values reduce ambiguity, guide people in setting direction and goals, and make it easier to hold one another accountable for decisions and actions. They keep people together and moving in the same direction.

A culture that says we can be whomever we please forfeits these capacities. We are left groundless on the shifting sands of changing identities. There is no communal ground to stand on.

So nobody stands for anything.

Because they trust themselves, they have no need to convince others by deception. Since their confidence has never deteriorated, they need not be fearful of others.

Chögyam Trungpa, Buddhist teacher

Western philosophy roughly divides ethics into three sorts[12]

The first, drawing on the work of Aristotle, holds that the virtues (such as justice, charity, and generosity) are dispositions to act in ways that benefit both the person possessing them and that person's society.

The second, defended particularly by Kant, makes the concept of duty central to morality: humans are bound, from a knowledge of their duty as rational beings, to obey the categorical imperative to respect other rational beings.

Third, utilitarianism asserts that the guiding principle of conduct should be the greatest happiness or benefit the greatest number.

"We are faithful; therefore we are not afraid."

I have worked with women religious (nuns and sisters) for more than twenty-five years. Shortly after the publication of *Leadership and the New Science* in 1992, a colleague gave me great advice. He said that if I was interested in organizations that worked from a strong sense of values, as I'd written about, then I should be working with the military and nuns. At the time it seemed an outrageous mix, but it was absolutely true. (You have already read of my work with the Army Chief of Staff, and in later chapters, you'll read two more stories that involve either the military or nuns.) What you read here are my personal descriptions and interpretations of events, not those of any of the sisters involved.

In 2012, acting on information gleaned from a doctrinal assessment, the Vatican exerted its patriarchal power in demanding that the Leadership Conference of Women Religious (LCWR) come into compliance with the doctrines of the Catholic Church. LCWR is the membership organization of sisters/nuns who lead the many orders and chapters of women religious in the United States. The Congregation for the Doctrine of the Faith (CDF) informed LCWR that "in order to implement a process of review and conformity to the teachings and discipline of the Church, the Holy See through the CDF will appoint an Archbishop delegate assisted by two bishops for review, guidance and, where necessary, approval of the work of LCWR." From my perspective, the women were being told to surrender their autonomy and come into obedience under Vatican rule.

LCWR functions like most professional associations in what they offer to 1,200 leader-nun members: retreats, seminars, mentoring, advisement, publications, lobbying, and an annual assembly that focuses their leadership on the world's most pressing needs. Just the titles of these assemblies are inspiring: *Embracing the Mystery: Living Transformation; Leadership Evolving: Graced, Grounded & Free; Springs of the Great Deep Spring Forth: Meeting the Thirsts of the World.*

I have spoken at two of these assemblies, most recently in 2016. The Vatican doctrinal assessment, with the Mandate for Implementation, seriously questioned the sisters' explorations of new cosmology, homosexuality, Christ in the world, and their choice of some of the speakers at these assemblies. So from the start, I had somewhat of a personal interest in how LCWR would respond. But much more important, over the years, I had developed deep relationships with several of the LCWR members. It was pure privilege to be in the background, walking with them as they undertook a three-year journey with patriarchal abuse, a journey that ended well because of many influences, including the atmosphere created by Pope Francis of inclusion and dialogue and their own reliance on contemplation and prayer as they sought direction. LCWR's journey was the steadiest and most enlightened embodiment of leading from integrity I have ever witnessed.

In late 2009, the Vatican began a different investigation of U.S. women religious, the Apostolic Visitation. All four hundred chapters or institutes of U.S. sisters were investigated by Vatican representatives (see Section Five: Perception, "A Tale of Two Stories"). These investigations began shortly after the revelations of the pedophilia scandals. As is common among leaders in trouble, they attempted to shift the spotlight off themselves and pivot attention onto the women. (The pedophilia scandals had already caused thousands of American Catholics who were still devoted to their faith to leave the official church and start home churches.)

———

Why the men in power ever thought this would work shows how blind they were: They believed they could act with total power and impunity when it came to the women of the church.

———

There were two separate investigations, aimed at different levels. The first series of investigations (described in Section Five) involved all women religious in the United States, more than 50,000 nuns and sisters. The second move by the Vatican was to insist that the more than 1,200 leaders of nuns and sisters come into obedience and docilely submit to Vatican control. So it was that in April 2012, the Vatican turned attention to the LCWR: they issued a doctrinal assessment that included their plans, a Mandate for Implementation. The first display of their blinding arrogance was how they issued the mandate. In April, the Leadership of LCWR (composed of three presidents—past, present, future—working as one and also the executive director) were at the Vatican for their annual visit; these were regular yearly meetings between the many offices of the Vatican and LCWR to strengthen relationships between the sisters and the Church.

Their most significant meeting was with a cardinal and the Congregation for the Doctrine of the Faith (a title that gives me the shivers). In this meeting, an eight-page document was read to them. The first pages delineated the doctrinal assessment (their failings), and the second half described the Mandate for Implementation, laying out a five-year process to bring them into compliance (i.e., obedience) with Church doctrine. The document was severely critical of the work they had been doing, even saying they had not been living as faithful Catholics. The four women were completely blindsided by this—it had come with no warning. And before they even had left the chamber, the Vatican released the mandate to the United States Catholic Conference of Bishops website.

These two acts—intentionally surprising the leaders and releasing it immediately to the world— completely backfired. Why the Vatican thought they could go public (before the leadership of LCWR could inform their members) and not incite a reaction is nearly beyond belief, but very revealing. (There were many times in the ensuing three years when it felt to me as an observer that certain men in the Vatican would have preferred the good old days of the Inquisition. Seriously.)

American and Catholics worldwide reacted in outrage. Over 800,000 emails and letters were sent to LCWR, and others were sent to the Church hierarchy. People treasured the nuns and their lives of dedicated service— some wrote of the gifts they had received from nuns in schools, hospitals, and service to the poor. The Vatican demands for orthodoxy dishonored all their contributions: their dedication to living a vowed life, doing Christ's work, serving the poor and suffering. Instead, the measure of their good work was to be their compliance with orthodoxy.

I can only describe their three-year journey as a walk in ever-deepening faith. The sisters were well prepared for this. A few years prior, in another difficult situation, one of them had responded to a challenge by voicing what now became their mantra: "We are faithful; therefore we are not afraid." Each time they encountered opposition, dealt with meanness, felt betrayed, stood their ground, became weary, it was their faith that supported them. And so it deepened and, in contemplation, showed them the way forward.

Leading with Integrity

LCWR's journey into increased faith-based integrity is a long and complex tale, filled with examples of extraordinary leadership. And grace. Here are just a few things I witnessed:

- Immediately, they created principles for how to move through this. They would not use the media; they would seek to be in respectful, open dialogue; they would never violate or compromise their integrity. They would act with respect, stay open to learning, seek to develop relationships of trust, and not succumb to the inherent disrespect and aggression of the demands coming at them. These principles stayed vital to their discernment processes during the entire three years.

- At the beginning, they knew they had to define the nature of this struggle: they were working on behalf of all women and men, not just sisters, who suffer from institutional abuse of power. They believed the "God of the Future" had called them to this work on behalf of oppressed people everywhere, especially women.

- They relied on their tradition and experience with contemplative practices. No decisions were made in haste. Prayer and contemplation were trusted to discern right action. This was true both for individual leaders and in meetings with their members.

- They had confidence in their professional skills—consensus building; canon law; theology; church history; politics; women's rights. They were the right ones to undertake this cause, and they undertook it willingly.

- They educated themselves, and then their members, to the complexities of trends and dynamics that had coalesced in the Mandate. They brought in a diverse group of experts—historians, theologians, civil and canon law—to help them discern how best to respond. From this information, they discerned possible scenarios that presented a range of actions, from compliance to the possibility they could no longer walk with the Church. During the summer months, regional meetings explored all of these possibilities in deep conversation and contemplation, so that when the members gathered for their assembly in August, they knew what was at stake and could offer their full support to the presidency to engage in negotiations.

- They never retreated into isolation but used the participative, consensus-building processes many sisters use. At every meeting, they received votes of confidence and the full support of their members to act as they deemed necessary. The levels of trust between their leaders and most U.S. nuns (over 40,000) was extraordinary. Today, now years later, the leaders continue to receive expressions of deep gratitude for what they accomplished and the contemplative approach they used.

- Their highly participative structures enabled them to slow down the process. They could make no decisions on their own; everything had to be brought to regular meetings of the national board and the annual assembly. Time was an ally, even more so after the change of popes. The intense struggles for power that erupted between the craving-for-control bishops and Pope Francis created more time for the women.

■ At the end of three years (it was to be a five-year process), the presence of Pope Francis, and the building of increased understanding through communication, served to bring everything to resolution. Agreements were reached that maintained the autonomy of LCWR. The fruits of working in respectful dialogue with all those involved resulted in LCWR's full participation in determining the final agreement. In a minor but significant act, both sides agreed that, following the press release of the final agreement, there would be a thirty-day period of silence, with no interviews to the press. (The LCWR presidents later noted what a gift it was to have this period of silence within the organization as well as with the outside world.)

After the conclusion of all this, Pope Francis unexpectedly welcomed the three presidents and their executive director into his chambers for a private audience. No one else was present except for the pope's translator. They spoke in honest conversation for nearly an hour; primarily, they shared the joy of working for the Gospel. The photos from that meeting are exceptionally moving to all who knew of the long struggle: Beautiful Benevolence welcoming the women leaders who had served their faith so well.

In 2015, Pope Francis declared the Year of Consecrated Life. He continues to welcome the sisters into meaningful conversations about the future of the Church. In June 2016, he issued a formal Constitution Statement on "Women's Contemplative Life" that includes this tribute:

> Dear contemplative sisters, without you what would the Church be like, or without all those others living on the fringes of humanity and ministering in the outposts of evangelization? The Church greatly esteems your life of complete self-giving.

LCWR is able to turn its full attention back to serving the cries of the world. Even during this period, LCWR continued its mission and service, developing its Call for 2015 to 2022. Here is how it begins:

> Standing on the rich history of our past and the communion present among us, we, the Leadership Conference of Women Religious, commit ourselves to seeking God who beckons to us from a future abundant in grace, full of challenge, and rich in possibility. … Affirming LCWR's mission and setting direction for the coming years, we embrace our time as holy, our leadership as gift, and our challenges as blessing.

IDENTITY: NOTES

[1] In a recent study of ancient cells, evidence suggests that bacteria, very soon after life began (about 500 million years into life's 4-billion-year history), already had the sophisticated cellular machinery that exists today. This is much earlier and quicker than previous theories. See "Bacteria Perfected Protein Complexes More Than 3.5 Billion Years Ago," www.sciencedaily.com/releases/2016/06/160609134243.htm.

[2] The latest UN figures on the global refugee and migrant crisis caused by climate change, conflict, environmental degradation, lack of employment, and other elements are much larger than originally thought. It is now estimated that up to 700 million people will be forced to migrate as refugees from their countries by 2050.

[3] The Linguistic Society of America predicts that of today's roughly 5,000 to 6,000 languages, within 100 years the number will almost certainly fall to the low thousands or even the hundreds. More than ever, communities that were once self-sufficient find themselves under intense pressure to integrate with powerful neighbors, regional forces, or invaders, often leading to the loss of their own languages and even their ethnic identity. See http://www.linguisticsociety.org/content/endangered-languages.

    Wade Davis, anthropologist, ethnobotanist, author, and filmmaker, notices that the Wisdom Keepers of a tradition, the elders, are dying at the rate of roughly one every two weeks. "We will be witnessing the loss of fully half of humanity's social, cultural and intellectual legacy. This is the hidden backdrop of our age." *The Wayfinders: Why Ancient Wisdom Matters in the Modern World*, pp. 2–3.

[4] Read the details of how we're manipulated online from a former Google designer of how to do it well: "How Technology Hijacks People's Minds," https://medium.com/swlh/how-technology-hijacks-peoples-minds-from-a-magician-and-google-s-design-ethicist-56d62ef5edf3#.z9xh4yaai.

[5] Teddy Wayne, "The End of Reflection," *New York Times*, June 11, 2016, nytimes.com/2016/06/12/fashion/internet-technology-phones-introspection.html.

[6] This term was coined in the late '70s and took hold as a definition by the late '90s. The term *identity politics* has been applied retroactively to varying movements that long predate its coinage. It is fraught with emotion, opposition, and criticism, as you might suspect and can observe daily now. See https://en.wikipedia.org/wiki/Identity_politics.

[7] Articles continue to appear on the motivation of young terrorists. Here are five from the summer of 2016:

Mark Mazzetti and Eric Schmitt, "In the Age of ISIS, Who's a Terrorist, and Who's Simply Deranged?" nytimes.com, July 17, 2016.

For a historical look at terrorists, with emphasis on Northern Island, see John Gray, "Excitement, Hatred and Belonging: Why Terrorists Do It," newstatesman.com, July 28, 2016.

Very chilling to read from Germany: Katrin Kuntz, "Islamic State: How the IS Trains Child Soldiers," spiegel.de July 29, 2016.

How imprisoning suspects facilitates radicalization: Noemie Bisserbe, "European Prisons Fueling Spread of Islamic Radicalism," wsj.com, July 31, 2016.

About U.S. terrorists: "'In-Betweeners' Are Part of a Rich Recruiting Pool for Jihadists," nytimes.com. September 22, 2016.

[8] Globally, suicide is the second-leading cause of death in young people, aged 15–29. The World Health Organisation (WHO) estimates that each year approximately one million people die from suicide, a global mortality rate of 16 people per 100,000 or one death every 40 seconds. It is predicted that by 2020 the rate of death will increase to one every 20 seconds.

[9] See Arthur Schlesinger, *The Disuniting of America: Reflections on a Multicultural Society* (New York: Norton, 1998).

[10] See https://en.oxforddictionaries.com/word-of-the-year/word-of-the-year-2016.

[11] In my book *A Simpler Way* (1996), I attributed this wonderful quote to Brother David Steindl-Rast. When someone asked him for the source of this, his office wrote me because they couldn't find it anywhere in his writings. I offer it here as a very good thought of unknown origin, inspired by Brother David.

[12] Apple's online dictionary.

3. INFORMATION

—

It's Better to Learn Than Be Dead

A living system does not need any information from outside to be what it is, but it is strictly dependent on outside materials in order to survive.

— Fritjof Capra

What Science Teaches

Information is the invisible lifeblood of all living systems. Everything that is visible as a shape or form at the material level exists because of the way information was processed. This is information's role: it provides the ingredients for life to organize itself into a living system capable of growth and adaptation. This function is in the word itself: in-formation.

A system's semipermeable boundary is its sense-making or information-processing function. Beyond the boundary there is always more data to process; chaos is the greatest creator of information—every moment is rich with newness. Using cognition, a living system decides what to pay attention to and how best to respond. From the booming buzzing confusion, everything alive makes sense for itself, transforming data into meaningful information. Cognition does not require a brain; even single-cell organisms such as slime mold learn and change in response to their environment.[1] Every living organism must have cognition because it is the only way life takes form, through organizing information. Without cognition there cannot be life.

——

Many biologists and philosophers now understand life as an energy process for transforming information into physical form.

——

This is evident in our bodies—we have a physical form in which the cells change their material, yet we continue to be the same because a healthy cell processes information into the same form.[2] (Cells create ill health when they process information differently, as in autoimmune diseases and cancers.) Information is the source of all growth and development in a living system.

———

Gregory Bateson, a brilliant social scientist, anthropologist, and a founder of Cybernetics, defined information as "that which changes us." The poet Stafford Beer wrote, "Information is a difference that makes a difference."

———

This is the role of information in living systems. But there is a second role in Information Theory, where information is defined mathematically as a unit of communication capable of being transferred. Until 1948, information transmission suffered from entropy; as it passed along wires, the original message became degraded because of noise and distance. In that year, Claude Shannon revolutionized communications by defining information as a precise mathematical unit, a bit. His simple equation, likened in importance to Einstein's, made it possible to quantify information with absolute precision so that a transmission of any kind would have zero message distortion. "The idea that something as nebulous as 'information' could be quantified, analyzed, and reduced to a mathematical formula attracted tremendous attention."[3]

Shannon's work gave birth to the Digital Age. All information now used in any communication form—text, phone, radio waves, computers, visual images—is reducible to the same unit, bits. And these bits are transmitted with virtually no loss of accuracy whatsoever. This has facilitated the explosion of digital capacities such as artificial intelligence that require tremendous computing power and cloud storage that can hold nearly unlimited amounts of data. And technology isn't close to reaching the Shannon Limit, where the speed of transmissions effects errors. Some estimate that the most sophisticated systems built to date for encoding and decoding only approach half of the Shannon Limit, which means that new technologies can be developed capable of processing masses of complex information at much greater speeds than now.[4]

This is one reason why those in technology are so wildly optimistic about the future.

What should we call this age we're living in?

There are so many choices: the digital age,
the information age, the internet age, the computer age,
the connected age, the Google age, the emoji age,
the cloud age, the smartphone age, the data age,
the Facebook age, the robot age, the posthuman age.

The more names we pin on it, the more vaporous it seems.
If nothing else, it is an age geared to
the talents of the brand manager.
I'll just call it *Now*.

Nicholas Carr, Utopia Is Scary

Information Makes a Difference

It's disturbing for me to notice how information has changed so dramatically since the first time I wrote about it in *Leadership and the New Science*. This was 1991, before the Internet, before smartphones, before we had begun to communicate at digital speed. I had just discovered that order was available without control, that information was the source of newness and creativity, that living systems were capable of ordering themselves into higher functioning if they remained open to information. Even chaos felt rich with possibilities. Leaders needed to understand these incredible opportunities and relax their grip on information. They needed to open the organizational channels, share information freely, and become friends with the ambiguity and chaos that breed new information. If they did all these things without fear or restraint, the self-ordering capacities of the Universe would kick in, and we would be given the "gift of a living universe, the gift of evolution, growth into new forms. Life goes on, richer, more creative than before."[5]

Wow.

I don't regret writing any of that; it was an accurate description that felt true at the time. Now my words are most useful as a *before and after* perspective. Those possibilities were real until information changed from communications among people to high speed transmissions delivered in cyberspace. Information still is a difference that makes a difference, but it is its mode of delivery that has made the most significant difference in reshaping, in-forming global culture.

If you're old enough, you may remember life before the Internet. If you're very old, never mind.

———

You may remember reading newspapers, articles, and books to get your information. You may remember being able to read for more than a few minutes and to remember what you read. You may remember conversations where you leisurely discussed ideas with friends and family over a meal. You may remember gathering with work colleagues for hours or even days to think about plans and strategies. You may remember the esteem in which we held science as the source of important factual information. You may remember when there were facts. And evidence that was used in making decisions.

That way of life vanished with high-speed delivery, universal access, and social media. This combination has created more than information overload. Social media servers may transmit information without error, but messages still deteriorate—into feelings, opinions, rumors, and conspiracies.

———

The clear transmission of facts and evidence becomes irrelevant in the hyperemotional space of social media.

———

Facts come from a world external to ourselves—namely, reality. Actually, that's the whole point. But in the social media world, they are either meaningless or threatening to the self we're constructing and protecting. The world can't help but degrade into "It's all about me." Deluged with information filtered through the lens of popular self, our internal monitoring causes the world to shrink: Did the news make me feel bad? Turn it off. Did that comment upset me? Blast the messenger. Did that criticism hurt me? Get depressed or strike back. This is the tragedy of self-reference where, instead of responding to information from the external environment to create an orderly system of relationships, the narrow band of information obsessively processed creates isolation, stress, and self-defense.[6] Focused internally, the outside world where facts reside doesn't have meaning.

Our communication with one another via the Web generates extreme reactions. Think about how small events take over the Internet because people get upset from a photo and minimal information. There doesn't have to be any basis in fact or any understanding of more complex reasons for why this event happened. People see the visual, comment on it, and viral hysteria takes over. Even when more context is given later that could help people understand the event, it doesn't change their minds. People go back to scanning and posting, and soon there is another misperceived event to get hysterical about. One commentator calls this "infectious insanity."[7]

When there is real information (facts and evidence), it can be used deliberately to misinform, arouse anger, and generate support. The phrase is "weaponized information." It describes the intentional use of lies, fabricated data, and half-truths to win people over. This has always been true in brand management and marketing—we expect to hear false claims about a product. But it is increasingly used by formal leaders and politicians as a strategy to deceive the opposition, win approval ratings and influence decisions. They know what they're saying is not true, but if it furthers their power, they do more of it. This is the post-truth era.

No longer is information a source of order; it is used intentionally to create disorder to benefit the leader. This is an ages-old practice that the Web facilitates beyond a leader's wildest dreams.

———

Of course, leaders have always manipulated information and lied to us. But the Internet changes the power of this practice by adding speed and intensity. The velocity of the message changes how the content is perceived and this intensifies the emotional response. There's no time to think, only to react. In the midst of battle, who can stop to consider facts? You might get killed if you get distracted for a minute by accurate information. (Of course, if you had accurate information, you wouldn't be on the battlefield to begin with.)

Evidence of the Web's impact on factual information is also obvious in investigative reporting. I've personally seen many instances where younger reporters go after a public figure or organization, creating a scandal where there is none just to get ahead. When their newsroom bosses are called to account for the lack of facts in a report, for the promulgation of rumors and misinformation, they usually brush it off by mumbling something about free speech. No one is holding these reporters accountable for accuracy and factual evidence; they have carte blanche to destroy good leaders if this makes a name for themselves. What is judged as "newsworthy" is the attention your piece gets. And the number of Tweets you do each day.[8]

Other journalists still determined to do in-depth reporting of important issues draw our attention to the fact that in-depth means time. Thorough investigations require time and money and the support of editors.

The Panama Papers, a devastating report on how political leaders and politicians hid billions in personal wealth offshore, was the product of one year's dedicated work among the International Consortium of Investigative Reporters; nearly 400 reporters from 80 countries assessed the content of 11 million documents.[9] Surely this is one of the great examples of collaborative investigative reporting. And the sheer volume of documents from so many countries required such collaboration.

Many people have commented on media bias, a valid, serious concern with the growth of media conglomerates led by owners who arrogantly publicize their bias. Their manipulation of facts and deliberately constructed ignorance of issues has contributed mightily to public cynicism about facts. And now we need to pay attention to Facebook since it's becomes the major news source for millions.[10]

———

In people's confusion about what is real, what is bias, what is fact, what is misinformation, combined with their indifference to discern one from another, it becomes easier to label everything as bogus, false, rigged.

———

It takes effort to discern what's really going on—it's easier to be cynical. This attitude is alarmingly evident among younger people who grew up in the Internet age and have no other frame of reference or experience in assessing the validity of information.

I believe that what has happened to information explains what has happened to science.[11]

People feel free to dismiss any scientific research as bias, mere opinion like everything else. Once labeled as opinion, people feel free to dismiss it if it conflicts with their already formed personal views.

——

They casually push it aside or label it as conspiracy—if they even take notice of it at all. Or companies pay a few greedy scientists to falsely refute the work of the majority of scientists. And Congress persecutes climate scientists.[12]

If we were still behaving as rational, information-seeking humans, as living systems intent on survival, there would be no question about climate change. Or the destructive environmental and health impacts from toxic products and polluted air. Or the massive amounts of evidence about the issues most affecting our survival: social, political, environmental.

But we're not acting rationally. We're myopically focused on the petty conflicts that keep a waning civilization from noticing the destructive forces already occupying their doorstep.

Courage is the capacity to confront what can be imagined.

Leo Rosten

Did Neurochemicals Cause the Crash of 2008?

Psychology is a well-attested way of displacing attention from social causes. After the economic crash of 2008, some psychologists concluded that the problem was not the banks but the brain. Wall Street had been afflicted by the wrong kind of neurochemicals. There was too much testosterone among traders, and too many bankers were high on cocaine. A drug was accordingly developed based on brain scans of traders that promised better decision making. What matters in the narcissistic world of late capitalism is not what you think or do but how you feel. And since how you feel can't be argued against, it is conveniently insulated from all debate. Men and women can now stroll around in continuous self-monitoring mode, using apps to track their changes of mood. The brutal, domineering ego of an older style of capitalism has given way to the tender self-obsession of the new.[13]

William Davies

How the Digital Age Destroyed the Information Age

The moment information changed from a sense-making relationship between a living system and its environment (i.e., the real world), the moment it moved into virtual reality, we were doomed to lose our best human qualities. We didn't lose our ability to discern and respond intelligently—we still do have brains. We forfeited these to machines that do it faster, with more hype, more allure, more seductions. We stopped being sense-making beings and succumbed to being senseless, distracted, not-quite-recognizable versions of what a human being is.

In 2012, in *So Far from Home,* I wrote about the impact of distraction on both our social interactions and the brain's physical changes caused by Internet use. I retold the story of the *Titanic* and the role of distraction in the sinking of the unsinkable. Less than an hour before the ship collided with the iceberg, the radio operator responded to warnings about ice in the area with "Shut up, shut up. I'm busy."[14]

As shocking as that story is, our levels of distraction have gotten so much worse since 2012 as we've ceded control to virtual worlds and put smartphones and tablets into the hands of everyone, including children. As far back as 2013 (and there's been an exponential rise in the use of these devices since then), the American Pediatric Association reported that children aged 8–10 were spending eight hours a day with various digital media; teenagers were spending eleven hours a day in front of screens. One in three toddlers were using phones and tablets before they could talk.[15] Since then, with ubiquitous smartphones (two-thirds of teens have them), a 2015 survey found that teens are on social media nine hours a day, and two-thirds of them do their homework while online with friends.[16]

These figures might not startle you (they should startle all of us) if you pause for a moment and notice your own behavior and that of the young people in your life. How often do you check your cell phone? (Reports vary from 80–150 times a day on the average.) How many screens do you and your family own? How long are you in a conversation before everyone suddenly is back staring at their phones?

———

It's hard not to notice the ubiquitous presence of smartphones and tablets now in every hand. I've imagined a visitor from outer space sculpting an image of the human body: one hand would be shaped as a small rectangular object.

———

You've probably also noted the impacts of virtual distraction on your own and others' behaviors: memory loss, inability to concentrate, being asked to repeat what you just said, miscommunication the norm, getting lost online and wasting time you don't have, withdrawing from the real world. The list of what's being lost is a description of our best human capacities—memory, meaning, relating, thinking, learning, caring. There is no denying the damage that's been done to humans as technology took over—our own Progress Trap.

The impact on children's behavior is of greatest concern for its present and future implications. Dr. Nicolas Kardaras, a highly skilled physician in rehabilitation, is author of *Glow Kids: How Screen Addiction Is Hijacking*

Our Kids—and How to Break the Trance. He describes our children's behavior in ways that I notice in my younger grandchildren: "We see the aggressive temper tantrums when the devices are taken away and the wandering attention spans when children are not perpetually stimulated by their hyper-arousing devices. Worse, we see children who become bored, apathetic, uninteresting and uninterested when not plugged in."[17]

These very disturbing behaviors are not just emotional childish reactions. Our children are behaving as addicts deprived of their drug. Brain imaging studies show that technology stimulates brains just like cocaine does. It is addictive because it increases dopamine levels (the "feel good transmitter") as much as drugs or sex. Numerous researchers now use terms such as "electronic cocaine," "digital heroin," and "digital pharmakeia (drugs)."[18]

———

From his experience, Dr. Kardaras notes "I have found it easier to treat heroin and crystal meth addicts than lost-in-the-matrix video gamers or Facebook-dependent social media addicts."

———

There are solutions for our children and ourselves if we ply ourselves away from screens and reestablish our relationship with the real world. It has been known for a long time that children's healthy development requires social interactions, imaginative play, and getting outside and engaging with the natural world. The same prescription has been proven true for us adults, as I hope you've noticed. The things that innately give us pleasure—nature, play, being together—are the sources for us to regain our intelligence, caring, and compassion.

———

As we engage with life in all its brilliance, our natural capacities can be restored. These capacities have never left us. We were the ones who unconsciously forfeited them.

———

We left them for distractions and enticements that have distanced us from each other and from what is real. As the world grows darker and distractions increase exponentially, we need to rediscover our innate human intelligence. Sane behavior requires that we reconnect with life, that we willingly and consciously seek out information, not more distractions.

Chögyam Trungpa, one of my Buddhist teachers, said, "Someone has to plant the seed so sanity can be restored."

I know he was talking about us.

I can calculate the motion of heavenly bodies, but not the madness of people.

Sir Isaac Newton

What Happened to Learning?

In biology, living and learning are synonyms, indistinguishable processes that keep life growing and moving forward. A living system is a learning system.

The good news is that more learning is going on now than ever before.

The bad news is that this learning is being done by machines. This is no sci-fi fantasy: machine learning, deep learning, and artificial intelligence have been growing exponentially since 2015.[19] How do you teach a machine to learn? You pretend it has a human brain.

To design machines that can learn, it is the human brain and our cognitive processes that provide the model. There isn't anywhere else to look for how complex learning takes place. The human brain is indecipherably complex, often described as a neural network. Twenty-five years ago, neural nets were a new way of understanding how the human brain functioned as exceedingly dense networks through which electrical activity stimulated connections. Memory, insight, behavioral responses happen as a result of connections across large regions of the brain as well as from one physical area being stimulated. However, if today you Google "neural networks," the citations are solely about machines: "A neural network is a computer system modeled on the human brain."

I rest my case. The machines have taken over.

And how many times do you hear people say, or perhaps say it yourself: "The human brain is a computer." Not true. Please do not repeat.

How did learning become a machine function? Simply because computers are faster at processing huge amounts of data. This is not information of the old-fashioned variety—ideas, knowledge, wisdom—but the brand-new *amazing* mathematical bits that can be measured, manipulated, and transmitted without error. Machines have much greater computational power for processing data, even as they model themselves on us. But it's important to keep clear the distinction between data and information.

———

We may think our machines are learning, but really, they're performing logical operations programmed to reduce huge amounts of data into ever more refined patterns and clusters. Assigning meaning to these can only be a human function: After all, meaning making is what defines us as human.

———

It's an eerie experience to learn about the field of artificial intelligence (AI), now appearing everywhere as the hottest field in tech R&D. It's unsettling because the terms used to describe machine learning are so human. Because AI has taken over and is the wave of our technological future, I go into some detail here. And if you are wondering why I know even a little about this emerging field that's hijacked learning, it's not because I'm a computer nerd. I'm the mother of a computer nerd who teaches data analytics at the university level and runs his own consulting firm.[20]

Machine learning involves pattern recognition and computational learning theory. It gives machines the ability to learn without being explicitly programmed. Algorithms for processing information allow the machine to learn from and make predictions from the data they process.

Algorithms embody the kind of logic we humans used in the old days: If this, then that. Cause and effect. Consequences.

———

At least that's my personal definition. The algorithm[21] provides a model for the machine's work; it uses the examples built into the model to process the data. There is *supervised* and *unsupervised learning* (these are technical terms). In supervised learning, the machine is given examples of behaviors that have been labeled by a human, at least for now.[22] Through *inductive bias* the computer uses these labels to identify and sort the data. (The definition notes that "The parallel task in human and animal psychology is often referred to as concept learning." I find this amusing.)

In unsupervised learning, the machine is tasked to make inferences without preset labels. This requires very sophisticated statistical methods only recently developed that feed on huge amounts of data. These methods have impressive names: choice-based conjoint; hierarchical clustering; anomaly detection; expectation-maximization algorithm; autoregressive integrated moving averages (ARIMA). These are all based on regression analysis, still recognized as "the king of statistics" (so my son tells me).

The newest field in AI is *deep learning*. This branch of unsupervised learning is required for voice, text, and visual recognition—human skills that we've come to expect in our phones, apps, and computers.

It is worth noting that machines require incredible levels of complexity to simulate these basic human behaviors, all of which we've been able to do since we were babies.

——

Andrew Ng founded and led a project at Google to build massive deep learning algorithms. "Loosely inspired" by our brains, his team built a highly distributed neural network, with over 1 billion parameters, working on 16,000 CPU cores (computers) to learn on its own (without human interference) how to identify cats on YouTube videos. This is a major achievement and signals great possibilities for the future for AI recognition systems.[23]

Yes, but … Is anybody noticing that it took 1 billion factors processed by 16,000 computers to simulate what babies do within a few months of birth? I suppose that doesn't matter, now that all this computing power is so cheap and available.

Machines are proving smarter at visual detection in some areas, especially in medical diagnostics, a field of professionals (i.e., people) being run ragged by patient loads, intense schedules, and exhaustion. Perhaps this is our future—we overwork people to the point where they make mistakes, accuse them of being inferior, and then justify replacing them with machines that don't get tired. And aren't human. Which medicine is still about—or should be.

This burgeoning field of data analytics can't help but get seduced by all its *amazing* numbers. It was bound to happen in our numbers-loving culture.

———

Awash in numbers that keep increasing in volume, possessing ever-greater calculative capacities, where are the analysts who know what to do with them once they get them? Very few analysts even think about context: Why do they get these results? What was going on in the people being surveyed? What is the meaning of their responses? So while number crunching has accelerated at digital speed, the meaning of the numbers remains obscured. And statisticians and scientists don't even understand some of their favored statistical processes.[24] So much data, so little meaning.

Most of us have experienced the tyranny of numbers; they've won the day as the only acceptable lens for describing what's going on in our bodies, our politics, our society. For decades, organizational leaders have had to bear the burden of measures that don't measure what's important. But now that data has assumed cult status and dashboards for number crunching are organizational must-haves, it's only going to get worse. It is estimated that in 75 percent of cases, leaders don't know what to do with the data they're given. This percentage is a familiar statistic in leadership studies that research other topics: the rate of failure of organizational change efforts, as reported by CEOs, is in this range.[25]

The sophisticated analytics, the charts, graphs, and dashboards, are *not* giving us information. They're submerging us with data. It is only information that makes a difference.

—

Accumulating more and more data without the interpretive lens that a living system relies on—its intelligence—doesn't give us learning. It does the opposite. It increases our confusion. And confused leaders can't make good decisions, no matter how much data they have.

Neural Networks Can Herd Cats

Picking images of cats out of YouTube videos was one of the first breakthrough demonstrations of deep learning.

Andrew Ng's breakthrough work at Google was to take neural networks and make them huge, increasing the layers and the neurons, and then run massive amounts of data through the system to train it. In Ng's case it was images from 10 million YouTube videos. Ng put the "deep" in deep learning, which describes all the layers in these neural networks.

Today, image recognition by machines trained via deep learning in some scenarios is better than humans, including identifying indicators for cancer in blood and tumors in MRI scans. In the Asian game of Go, Google's AlphaGo defeated Korean Go master Lee Sedol in five matches. It learned the game and trained for its Go match—it tuned its neural network—by playing against itself over and over and over.[26]

After the match, the official Korean Go (Paduk) Association awarded AlphaGo the highest Go grandmaster rank—an "honorary 9 dan"—in recognition of AlphaGo's "sincere efforts" to master Go.[27]

When did machines become sincere?

Restoring Learning to Decision Making

I don't think I need to convince you of the need for learning and its powerful impact on decision making. Many of us were deeply inspired by Peter Senge's concept of the Learning Organization. The effectiveness of processes that create learning is beyond question and well documented in books that describe processes for individual, team, and organizational learning. Organizations and their leaders have proven how powerful it is to learn from experience and apply this to decisions and actions. Without question, organizations become more creative, effective, and resilient. And individuals and teams who engage in learning are much more innovative, engaged, and work well together in trusted relationships. Without question. We know this.

I admit that every time I've spoken about the need to bring learning from experience back into organizational decision making, I've felt ridiculous. Really?! We don't know this is essential to our survival!? C'mon, people....

The greatest enemy of thinking is busyness (business?). I used to love a Zen teacher's comment that the Western form of laziness is to be busy, while Asian laziness is too much meditation. But I don't think that's true any longer. Busyness isn't our way of avoiding things—it's our total and complete lifestyle. We have too much to do, too many responsibilities, too many kids' activities—and in this deluge of tasks and to-dos, we're highly distracted. With distracted minds, we can't remember what we were supposed to do next. And we don't have the brain power to do that well, whatever that was.

I'm assuming you've had direct experience with the power of learning to support wise decisions and how, within a team, learning transforms troubled relationships into creativity and support. As you recall these experiences, as either a leader or participant, take a moment to remember what it felt like when thinking and learning were commonplace.

When thinking falters, a living system is at risk. If it continues unchecked, the organism dies. Think about it.

Now you know what to do.

Even capable and honest leaders have no viable way forward. Although the problems may be insoluble, something must be done, and since expediency no longer suffices, they resort to stupidity— doing what has never worked in the past, what cannot succeed in the present, and what will destroy the future both morally and practically.

Joseph Tainter

What Does Human Being Mean?

How do you measure the expense of an erosion of effort and engagement, or a waning of agency and autonomy, or a subtle deterioration of skill? You can't. Those are the kinds of shadowy, intangible things that we rarely appreciate until after they're gone, and even then we may have trouble expressing the losses in concrete terms. But the costs are real. The choices we make, or fail to make, about which tasks we hand off to computers and which we keep for ourselves are not just practical or economic choices. They're ethical choices. They shape the substance of our lives and the place we make for ourselves in the world. Automation confronts us with the most important question of all: What does human being mean?

Nicholas Carr, Utopia Is Freaky

The Origin of a Great Line

I am sitting in a dusty café in the middle of nowhere—Fort Irwin, where the Army trains soldiers in tank warfare. This is a stark, endless desert linking Nevada and California. We flew in by helicopter. I am having coffee with a colonel whose name I don't remember, but whose comments I remember with the clarity of today, even though this was in 1993.

We have been up before dawn to travel to a high hill that offers a panoramic view of everything going on for more than fifty miles. It's a vast and desolate landscape. But we're focused on what's going on below us, at the base of the hill where well-worn tracks weave in and out of low hills and sand dunes. We are observing tank warfare, hundreds of tanks engaged in mock battle, a training event. There is no live ammo; if you're ambushed, your computer screen tells you you're dead or wounded and how badly. Even with my untrained eye, I can see tanks getting into trouble, unable to save themselves from death and injury. The number of casualties keeps growing.

The base commander, a general, is walking around rubbing his hands in glee: "Lots of learning going on down there, lots of learning!"

Later in the morning, I observe an After Action Review (AAR), a process invented by the Army in the late '70s and still used not only by the military, but by other federal agencies, police forces, even a few corporations. A great deal has since been written about this process. This morning is one of my first experiences with this now famous process. I'm standing with about twelve soldiers and their captain at the back of a truck. They're trying to figure out where things went wrong, why and how they got killed in the morning battle. They've been trained in the AAR process and use it after every battle, mock or real.

I've since observed this process many times, sometimes in rooms with only blackboards, sometimes in formal settings with screens and technology. But here, it was a group of very tired soldiers at the back of a truck, trying to learn from what just happened. I remember the intensity of the conversation—I can't recall whether anyone was taking notes. I remember the heat and the dust. I remember the energy of everyone as they voiced comments and ideas in rapid fire exchanges. No doubt they wanted to get back to the base, get some breakfast, take a shower. No doubt, at this moment, they were fully engaged in figuring out how not to mess up the next time.

Later, sitting in the cafe with the colonel, I blurted out that I had never seen so much learning going on. I'd been in many organizations, in many different circumstances, but I'd never seen a leader even faintly enthusiastic, let alone rubbing his hands in glee, about the amount of learning he was witnessing with all the mistakes going on. And I'd never experienced the energy and focus at the back of that truck. I consolidated all these experiences to the colonel in one statement: "The Army is the first and only true learning organization I've ever seen." (Twenty-five years later, I've only encountered a few others and none come close.)

He smiled, apparently delighted with the comparison. Then he replied quietly, "Well, Meg, we figured that one out a long time ago. It's better to learn than be dead."

The Principles and Process of an After Action Review (AAR)

AARs are used by a number of federal agencies that deal with crises such as wild fires and natural disasters. Police forces also use them after significant incidents. I've worked with a few organizations who relied on this process after a crisis, including the National Park Service and a few corporations.

Any incident is an extraordinary opportunity for learning, not only relevant to the incident, but also about the organization's culture. How well did we communicate? Where did trust or distrust factor in? Were our values evident in our behaviors?

I love this process for what it yields in terms of actionable learning. Its entire focus is on performance and learning how to do things better. I love it even more because it brings a system together in its diversity of people, roles, and ranks and treats everyone with respect for their contribution. It is the diversity of perceptions that creates genuine insight. And the participatory process of an AAR guarantees that learning will be quickly implemented. People want to contribute and learn; we support what we create. The AAR process uses these internal motivators when we need them most—at a time of crisis, when something's gone wrong. In this time of never-ending crises, this is a healthy and reliable process.

Core Elements of an AAR

- Priority is given to this process. No matter what, time is made available to learn from the crisis or situation.

- Everyone who was part of the action or crisis is present and expected to contribute.

- Rank and hierarchy don't matter: it is acknowledged that everyone has something of potential value to contribute.

- The process is disciplined. Specific questions are asked in order. Facilitation is needed to ensure that only one question is answered at a time and that each person speaks without being contradicted or challenged.

- Learnings are recorded in some form. They are available as lessons learned for the benefit of others.

- The value of learning is visible in consequent actions. People feel smarter and gain confidence that they can deal with the next crisis.

The Four Questions of an AAR

To be asked in this order:

1. *What just happened?* Everyone offers a personal description; no one is challenged on whether their description is accurate. Widely divergent descriptions give the most information.

2. *Why do you think it happened?* People offer their interpretations, again without being challenged. Then these are explored for their diversity and commonalities. This exploration usually reveals a great deal of information beyond the incident. The culture becomes visible, especially around hierarchy, communications, and trust.

3. *What can we learn from this?* Here is where the richness of diverse perceptions can be shaped into learning outcomes that build on the complexity of the situation rather than overly simplified analyses.

4. *How will we apply these learnings?* Specific actions, defined outcomes, specified work, and a motivated team—all possible because of this good process.

Dealing with the Impossible

Jim Varghese, a brilliant executive leader in Australia, told me a story of doing something I had only dreamed should be done: he locked managers in a room until they came up with a solution. Years ago, I had thought this might get the U.S. Congress back on track but, as things deteriorated, even this seemed fanciful. Now, if left to themselves, it'd be an episode of the reality TV show *Survivor*. Or worse.

I worked with Jim over many years as he occupied several different senior-level leadership positions, first as director general (chief executive) of three different departments within the Queensland Australia government, and then as CEO of Springfield Land Corporation, building the largest planned city in Australia and tenth largest in the world. (I watched this city rise from empty land, using progressive principles to create health and community; it was astonishing to see it become real and made my own work, at the time focused on relationships to "build healthy communities," seem very easy by comparison.)[28]

At the time he implemented the lock-down technique, Jim was director general of Main Roads in Queensland. One day, his staff of engineers approached him with terrible news. They could not complete the road because they'd run into problems with the land on which the next portion of road needed to go. There was no alternative route, the road was partially built, and already hundreds of millions had been spent on this project. But now, the engineers insisted, there was no recourse but to abandon the project.

For many years before and after this incident, Jim had a strong track record of using learning circles as a collaborative thinking process even for the most difficult issues. In later years, as director general of Primary Industries and Fisheries, he would be faced with the economic and human havoc wreaked by the Category 5 hurricane Larry that devastated the north Queensland coast. I remember seeing photos of banana trees laid on their side—the total destruction of a fruit industry. He told me that, right after the hurricane struck and they knew the extent of the devastation, their first commitment was to ensure they responded well, unlike the U.S. government had done after Katrina.

And there were many other crises that Jim had been told were impossible to solve, including how to contain the spread of equine flu virus in the horse country of Queensland (he was publicly ridiculed for thinking he could stop it. But he did.) His reliable strategy always was to bring together everybody who had a stake in the issue, make sure they came well prepared and ready to offer their data and insights, expect to enrich the information through probing exchanges, together make sense of the crisis, and then determine a response or solution. He also introduced learning circles to a remote Aboriginal community; over years of use, this collaborative thinking process has transformed their relationships and decision making.

I knew Jim to be dedicated to reflection and learning, both personally and as a leader. During a change of governments in his younger years, he'd been laid off for 3.5 months not knowing when/if he'd return to his government post. Already with considerable experience in leadership, he used that period to reflect on what he had learned. This period of deep reflection (with gardening) resulted in what I call a coherent theory of action. Jim calls it the "Three Learning Frames," a process for aligning purpose and objectives with relationships, structures, and systems.[29]

No matter which leadership position he held, Jim knew what to pay attention to based on his theory of action. He also knew to engage people to solve their own problems, whether technical or social. And he had complete confidence in the power of reflection and learning.

———

Back to the engineers locked in a room. Jim would not take no for an answer—he might have been fired if the road ended there and the project failed, but his motivation was not based on self-protection. He believed that, under pressure, the engineers could find a solution. And they did. (Recall that scene in *Apollo 13* where the mission commander dumps on the table all the parts available on the spacecraft and tells the engineers to jerry-rig a solution and get the crew home. "Failure is not an option.")

There is another maxim, "Necessity is the mother of invention." But even in the face of necessity, how often do we rely on bringing people together, pooling all the information, expertise, and experience they have, and trust that if we keep them together in a good collaborative process that they'll come up with an answer? It's one thing to refuse to take "no" for an answer, but it's quite another to have the faith that if you hold the right people together in collaborative discovery mode, they will find a workable solution.

———

In my experience, in the face of imminent failure, most leaders draw inward and disappear from view.

They may be consulting a few trusted advisors or lawyers. Or moving their wealth offshore. Or deny the problem and leave us to fend for ourselves. Each of these behaviors have been well rehearsed in other civilizations in the same stage of decay.

Jim offers the alternative: Gather diverse people together, trust that they each have useful information, get the experts involved as partners, hold them together, use the pressure of time to push them, but also don't unnecessarily rush them. And only then unlock the door. (I mean this figuratively, as Jim only did this one time. But it's true that people have to feel the pressure of no exit.)

Most of the time, Jim's approach results in workable solutions. And even when it doesn't, people emerge with stronger, more trusting relationships, the ultimate resource we need in hard times.

Please note: I know you're smart enough to see the difference, but I feel compelled to note that this strategy of insisting on a solution is nothing like and completely different from the common practice of setting unreachable sales and production goals and then, when people do reach their targets, raising the ceiling again. Then again.[30]

INFORMATION: NOTES

[1] See http://www.abc.net.au/news/2016-04-27/slime-mould-can-learn-even-without-brain/7363176?site=science/news.

[2] Cells in our liver change every six weeks, in our brains every twelve months. Margaret Wheatley. *Leadership and the New Science,* 3rd ed., p. 95.

[3] MIT Technology Review, https://www.technologyreview.com/s/420369/code-quest/.

[4] See http://searchnetworking.techtarget.com/definition/Shannons-Law

[5] *Leadership and the New Science,* 3rd ed., p. 112.

[6] In a report on British girls, "More than a third of girls aged 10 to 15 years old are unhappy with their appearance and a quarter are unhappy with their lives." *How do you help young girls feel happier?* Emma Thelwell, bbc.com August 23, 2016.

[7] Under the headline "infectious insanity," the editor-in-chief of *Die Welt*, Stefan Aust, wonders whether social media and the Internet have helped violence become "virally transmitted like common flu". http://www.bbc.com/news/world-europe-36882525

[8] For a penetrating, scathing report on the state of journalism (with enough irony and humor to see clearly), watch John Oliver's TV show *Last Week Tonight*, August 7, 2016, https://www.youtube.com/watch?v=bq2_wSsDwkQ.

[9] The Panama Papers revealed how at least twelve political leaders (including Putin) and 143 politicians hid billions of dollars in offshore accounts. How much of these funds were stolen from public coffers? https://www.theguardian.com/news/2016/apr/03/what-you-need-to-know-about-the-panama-papers. Information on the work of the reporters in the International Consortium is found here: https://www.propublica.org/podcast/item/Meet-the-Panama-Papers-Editor-Who-Handled-376-Reporters-in-80-Countries

[10] Note the U.S. logo created out of emojis. Brilliant. http://www.nytimes.com/2016/08/28/magazine/inside-facebooks-totally-insane-unintentionally-gigantic-hyperpartisan-political-media-machine.html

[11] Among many excellent writings about the denigration of science, see Dan Rather's piece in *Scientific American*, November 2016, https://blogs.scientificamerican.com/guest-blog/dan-rather-now-more-than-ever-we-must-stand-up-for-science/.

[12] The harassment of climate scientists, from Congress, right-wing media, and conspiracy theorists has necessitated the creation of a legal defense fund for climate scientists: http://climatesciencedefensefund.org/.

[13] *The Happiness Industry* by William Davies, reviewed by Terry Eagleton. "Why Capitalism Has Turned Us into Narcissists." theguardian.com August 3, 2016.

[14] Margaret Wheatley, *So Far from Home*, p. 87.

[15] Dr. Nicholas Kardaras, "It's Digital Heroin: How Screens Turn Kids into Psychotic Junkies," *New York Post*, August 27, 2016. http://nypost.com/2016/08/27/its-digital-heroin-how-screens-turn-kids-into-psychotic-junkies/.

[16] Survey was done by Common Sense Media.

[17] Kardaras, "It's Digital Heroin."

[18] Ibid. This article is well worth reading, as is Kardaras's book, *Glow Kids*.

[19] This sudden growth is attributed to nearly infinite storage on the Cloud, exceedingly fast computing power, and lowered costs.

[20] Check it out at www.emperitas.com.

[21] The words *algorithm* and *algorism* come from the name al-Khwārizmī. Al-Khwārizmī (Persian: c. 780–850), a Persian mathematician, astronomer, geographer, and scholar. https://en.wikipedia.org/wiki/Algorithm.

[22] In November 2016, Google reported that one of their AI systems had created its own encryption system. The humans couldn't penetrate it.

[23] http://www.andrewng.org/portfolio/deep-learning-and-unsupervised-feature-learning/.

[24] "Not Even Scientists Can Easily Explain P-values." http://fivethirtyeight.com/features/not-even-scientists-can-easily-explain-p-values/.

[25] This rate of failure in change initiatives has stayed depressingly stable at about 70 percent since the first studies done in the mid-1990s. From my direct observations, I personally think the rate is even higher. See http://www.gallup.com/businessjournal/162707/change-initiatives-fail-don.aspx.

26 http://www.andrewng.org/portfolio/deep-learning-and-unsupervised-feature-learning/.

27 https://en.wikipedia.org/wiki/AlphaGo_versus_Lee_Sedo.

28 Now at 32,000 residents with public transport, a university, schools, hospital, sports complex, shopping mall, and much more, designed for 138,000 residents. http://www.greaterspringfield.com.au/.

29 For more on Jim Varghese, see https://mindhive.org/people/-25.

30 A tragic example that also sheds a light on the pressures set by American corporations in India and elsewhere is "Driven to Suicide by an 'Inhuman and Unnatural' Pressure to Sell," *New York Times*, August 11, 2016. In the United States, in September 2016, the largest American bank, Wells Fargo, was fined $185 million for the practice of faking millions of new accounts in order to meet sales targets and look good to Wall Street. At the time, before pressured by Congress, they fired no senior leaders, but the executive in charge retired with a $100 million plus retirement package. They did fire 5,300 staff who had felt they had no choice but to falsify sales. The CEO resigned when all this became public.

4. SELF-ORGANIZATION

Order for Free

The world is not to be put in order, the world is order. It is for us to put ourselves in unison with this order.

— Henry Miller, playwright

What Science Teaches

Everything alive forms nothing into something by creating an identity for itself. This is the dynamic of self-organization—life's capacity to create order from chaos, to create growth and potential where there was none. The process of self-organizing is in the term itself: There is a self that gets organized.

Living systems are self-organizing; they exchange information with their environment and use that information to adapt to changed conditions. Information is filtered through their identity, determining what's relevant and what's not. All of life possesses the essential freedom to decide what to pay attention to and how to respond to what they just noticed.

—

Without the filter of identity, there can be no sense making and no living system. With a clear identity, the system develops, adapts, and creates new capacities.

—

Chaos science adds another dimension to the biological with *Strange Attractors*.[1] These are shapes of mesmerizing beauty that appear on a computer screen as a chaotic system displays its behavior over millions of iterations. Each point on the screen is the sum of a complex equation. It may land far or near to the preceding one, but all behavior is held within a "basin of attraction." This basin is created from the nature of the equation—it is self-referencing, continually feeding back on itself. One sum feeds immediately into the next; every point is different, based on an equation where each result is new, and then used in the next calculation.[2]

The order inherent in chaos becomes beautifully visible as a shape or pattern. If each individual moment is charted in two dimensions, it looks like disorder, lines going up and down forever. Adding a third dimension, as is true in life, reveals these astonishing patterns of deep order and harmonious beauty. This is an important discovery that applies to both inanimate and animate systems—their behavior becomes visible as patterns as they interact in a network of connections.

The conditions necessary to create this order are so minimal that complexity scientist Stuart Kauffman termed this "order for free." A few set of rules that are self-referencing, operating autonomously, unconstrained by any other controls, will instantaneously establish an orderly pattern of behavior.[3]

The ordering capacity of this Universe restores the original meaning of "awesome."

When Humans Self-Organize

We live with the most powerful vehicle for self-organizing ever known on this planet: the Internet. It is possible to find anything, connect with anybody, and organize groups around their interests at ever more discrete levels of personalization. And all of this within a matter of seconds. In the early days, this freedom to organize was intoxicating and exciting. We found new ideas, information, support—the World Wide Web was inviting and spacious. The Web was able to grow so quickly and extend its reach everywhere because it made excellent use of the dynamic of self-organization.

The Web still provides all that, but now at a high price of incessant marketing, daily petitions for myriad social causes, fund-raising efforts from unknown groups, scams, frauds—this is easy to observe any morning when overnight emails download. And the tone of these emails is increasingly loud, angry, and desperate—no wonder they're termed email "blasts" that we "shoot" at one another. Now that we've lived with Web 2.0 for a decade, its negative effects are clearly evident, and many thoughtful commentaries have appeared in the past few years.[4]

———

With us humans, self-organization is far more complex than with other living systems. It is complicated because we have high powers of cognition (or so it has been reported).

We don't just take in information from the environment—we use our brains to make up our own. Gossip, rumors, slander, lies, conspiracy theories—these fly around the Web at the speed of light.

This "information" is used to strengthen the group's identity. The system quickly closes in on itself. It becomes less in touch with the outer world, except to identify it as a threat. This is the trajectory of human self-organized efforts that is predictable from the start. The identity that first called people together intensifies, rigidifies, and pushes out divergent views; what was a permeable boundary becomes a wall of defense against outside hostile forces.

———

One reason identities slam shut is that other greater human needs supersede openness, curiosity, and intelligence. We need to belong. We need to feel accepted.

———

When we do belong, life is better, even healthier. People who work together in groups are happier than those who isolate themselves. The harder the work becomes, the more we bond together. We worry less about each other and how they irritate us and focus more on getting work done on behalf of the cause and defining enemy.[5] We have more energy for the work, greater dedication to our cause.

But as people become anxious to be accepted by the group, their personal values and behaviors are exchanged for more negative ones. We can too easily become more intense, abusive, fundamentalist, fanatical—behaviors strange to our former selves, born out of our intense need to belong.

This may be one explanation for why the Internet, which gave us the possibility of self-organizing, is devolving into a medium of hate and persecution, where trolls[6] claiming a certain identity go to great efforts to harass, threaten, and destroy those different from themselves.

The Internet, as a fundamental means for self-organizing, can't help but breed this type of negative, separatist behavior. Tweets and texts spawn instant reactions; back and forth exchanges of only a few words quickly degenerate into comments that push us apart. Listening, reflecting, exchanging ideas with respect—gone.

But this is far less problematic than the way the Internet has intensified the language of threat and hate. People no longer hide behind anonymity as they spew hatred, abominations, and lurid death threats at people they don't even know and those that they do. Trolls, who use social media to issue obscene threats and also organize others to deluge a person with hateful tweets and emails, are so great a problem for people who come into public view that some go off Twitter, change their physical appearance, or move in order to protect their children.[7] Reporters admit that they refuse to publish about certain issues because they fear the blowback from trolls.

It is important to understand both the power of self-organizing and its damaging effects because, still, it is the most powerful organizing dynamic we have. As leaders choosing to take a stand against these behaviors and to create the conditions for people to act with sanity, we need to know the full story about self-organization as it is manifesting in our culture.

In Britain, an analysis in 2015 by the think tank Demos found that on average, around 480,000 racial slurs are tweeted every month, compared to just 10,000 three years ago. The researchers admit that the vast majority of those uses won't amount to hate crimes. But the numbers are still significant. "A 4800 per cent increase is astonishing— far greater than the general increase in tweets over that time."[8]

"2015: The Year That Angry Won the Internet"

BBC News

"2015 saw a greater normalization of hate speech in society than in previous years," says Andre Oboler, chief executive of the Australia-based Online Hate Prevention Institute. "Where previously a person might make a vague negative allusion to race, religion, gender or sexuality, by the end of 2015 the comments on social media were blatant and overt."

People no longer felt the need to hide behind pages and fake accounts; "by the end of 2015 many people felt their hate was acceptable and were comfortable posting it under their real name or their regular social media account."

Oboler flagged up anti-Muslim hate as a particular hot spot— perhaps predictable considering the continued fallout of the Syrian civil war, the refugee crisis, and terror attacks. But other groups have also been among the top targets, he says, including women and Jews.

BBC News[9]

The Unstoppable Rise of Terror

In 2005, I wrote about terrorist groups as a prime example of self-organization.[10] They recruited young men, brainwashed them to be passionate about the cause, and then unleashed them to do whatever harm they could. In that essay, I was critical of the role of formal high commanders and the U.S. strategy of targeting leaders as the means to fight terrorism. Now, the increasing number of individual and small-group terrorist attacks all over the world prove that the strategy of independent actors wreaking hell wherever they can is growing in force and will continue to destabilize and terrorize us.[11]

But more information has come forth, offering detailed descriptions about the founding and ongoing organization of ISIS. These details come from men who identified themselves as loyal and devoted members to the cause of ISIS: to destroy Western civilization and achieve worldwide control as Muslims.[12] They left or were willing to reveal details of ISIS's inner workings because they became disgusted with what one called "the crazies" from Europe who had no religious basis and eagerly participated in violence that "has become too extreme … such things as crucifying, burning, and drowning its opponents and those who violate its rules."[13] In another case, it was the beheading of prisoners in order to create training videos, where the executioners questioned their best camera angle.[14] This may strike us as darkly ironic, but it's also instructive: it reveals that there can be limits to people's indoctrination and training—sometimes their deeper humanity pierces through.

ISIS has organized itself in three forms: as a theocratic state, as a hierarchical military force, and as self-organizing individual jihadists. Even as members of ISIS are defeated as a state and as a military, it is the increasing numbers of young people, spurred on by their alienation, enraged at the death of their leaders and ongoing military strikes, that will continue to wreak uncontrollable terror upon our world.

In the face of this reality, we can choose for our humanity or collapse in fear.

A relief worker for Mercy Corps in Syria commented that, as the bombs were going off near where she was delivering aid, "I didn't feel fear. I felt dignity."

Selfies

The beautiful bodies painstakingly trained
to be objects of admiration
are taking photos of themselves on the beach.

Any one of them could be
the handsome man smiling with his love
in that Instagram he sent
from the Bataclan before
he became an hour later one of many bloodied bodies
people clambered over to escape.

The Great Flaring Forth is
how some name the new story of the
Universe and its Big Bang birth
but now it's our story
as we flare up wildly
flinging fear
that disinters our lives into
terrors no longer remote
from those on the beach
posing in their perfection.

Margaret Wheatley
Written after the Paris attacks, November 2015,
at Bondi Beach, Sydney, Australia

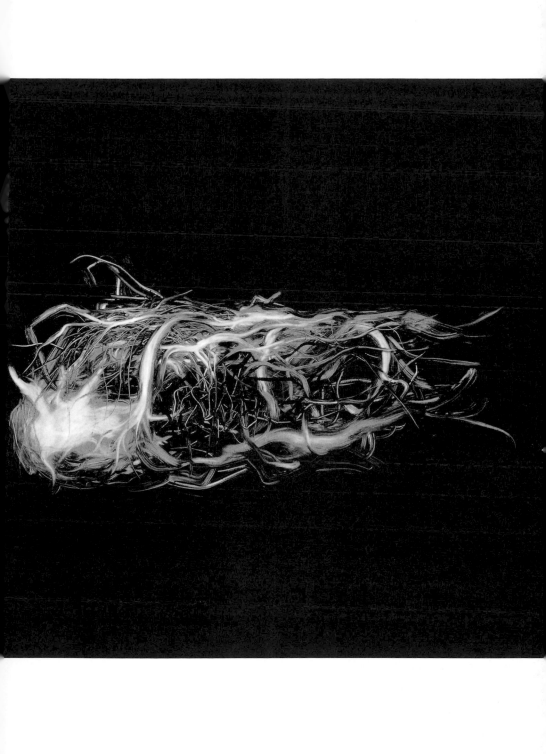

Leading with Self-Organization: Social Movements and Terrorism

These are indeed strange bedfellows; I hesitated to put them in the same title. But each of them compels our attention as significant players at this time in our history. In the pattern of collapse, the civilization is invaded by those set to destroy it and they eventually succeed; then they are the next ones to rise and collapse. This is the unalterable cycle that we humans create for ourselves.

———

Within the cycle of moral decay, there are always those few in number who choose to notice the loss and degradation. They stand up to preserve the values and behaviors from an earlier era, before decadence took hold.

———

They seek to preserve and illuminate these values, knowing they cannot prevent the devastation and unraveling. They give themselves wholeheartedly to prove that, in any circumstance, we humans can be generous, creative, and kind. I am calling their efforts islands of sanity.

This term *island* may be too physical a way to describe these (but I'm fond of it). Sometimes it is an identifiable space such as a geographic community, a small organization, or a department within a large organization. It's wonderful when the boundaries are so clear. Yet for many, it's an interior space bounded by our values, commitment, and faith. This boundary is only visible in our actions; no matter where we are, we stand out as different, leading against the norm. We aren't intent on changing the world; we simply try to work in ways that honor people and evoke our best human qualities.

All self-organized efforts, no matter their purpose, require leadership. Yet calling for formal leadership in self-organized networks is near to heresy.[15]

Self-organization creates networks, and networks have no hierarchy, just nodes or hubs. Therefore, hierarchy plays no role or, worse yet, is dangerous to the network's effectiveness. Leaders come from within the network—leadership emerges from the initiative of individuals and groups.

All of this is true, except for the fact that we humans interfere. The identity doesn't stay open, supporting people to be creative and contribute. It closes in, driven by other human needs for power, control, and attention. This is easily seen in any values-based organization such as nonprofits, religious organizations, spiritual communities. Greater orthodoxy increases over time: there's only one right way to do something, only one way to think. The system closes down as people's intense desire to serve their cause mixes with ego and fatigue. Tired people take the path of least resistance and just do what they've always done.

You may have experienced this sad trajectory many times, but you may not have experienced the type of leadership that can skillfully reverse the shutdown and open the system to new possibilities and ways of acting.

In a living system, continual interactions with the outside prevent the system from rigidifying. Yet the boundary of identity creates a basin of attraction so nothing wanders off too far as the system continues to adapt and survive.

———

But with humans, identity alone can't play this role; we have too many other needs and emotions. It takes a good leader to notice what's happening and work actively to avoid further solidification. Please don't read this as a prescription for command and control, although you've probably seen this happen: the organization is in high conflict with itself, and a well-meaning former corporate executive steps in to exert control and restore order. But this never works for long. The organization doesn't need more rigid controls—it needs a more focused identity that opens to new people and new ways of thinking.

It's troubling to say this, but the formal leaders of terrorist organizations know how to work with the process of self-organizing better than we do. They know how to generate fanatical commitment to a cause.

They provide online training materials that give individuals and groups the skills they need anywhere in the world. They kindle a great fire of hatred and then release people, placing no boundaries on individual acts of terror. Pursue anything and everything that kills "the Crusaders"— a stone, a knife, a gun, a truck to mow down more than one hundred people celebrating their freedom. Hatred is the orthodox identity, and the methods of destruction are the arena for individual creativity.

Beyond recoiling in horror from this perverse example, it would be good to understand how self-organized networks succeed with the right kind of leadership. Such leaders skillfully take advantage of self-organization by arousing individual creative acts that further the cause.

———

How leaders define success—for preservation or destruction, for peace or violence—depends on where they locate themselves in the pattern of history.

Leadership Lessons from Social Movements

It seems these days that our world is filled with movements. So many people call their work a movement if it engages a large group on the Internet; commentators casually apply the term to a group of people getting together in common cause for only an afternoon.

But you can't call your work a movement just because you have a lot of followers, or thousands of people have listened to your TED talk. A movement is not defined in numbers, although that's our beloved measure of popularity and success.

———

A movement is defined by the people willing to stay dedicated to their cause for a long time, those who take risks, work hard, expect defeat, and still keep going.

———

A true movement must have the strength and capacity for enduring over time: Mandela's autobiography was titled *Long Walk to Freedom*. Above all, movements must endure hardships and setbacks for very long periods and mourn together as gains disappear in the Age of Decadence. This is why so many of them refer to their work as "The Struggle." The South African struggle against apartheid lasted nearly a full century, from early 1900 to the election of Mandela in 1994.[16]

In the history of social reform, movements have accomplished their work through the combination of self-organization and charismatic leaders. Whether their purpose is to create reform, rebellion, or revolution, they are self-organizing at the beginning. They engage people's passions and hopefully their intellect, but it varies. Sometimes people just want to get out and protest; sometimes they offer a detailed critique of root causes of an issue; sometimes they seek to embody new values and ways of being as they protest the old ways. But to endure for the long road ahead, sane leadership is essential.

Those who have led movements have a great deal to teach those of us now setting out to create islands of sanity. We differ in our purpose and desired outcomes, but we are each standing up against the dominant culture. We are all working diligently to create possibilities for human beings to behave far better than the current culture influences us.

I have witnessed and learned from some great movement leaders: working in South Africa during the golden age of Mandela; learning from friends leading the Farmworkers Union; experiencing close hand the work in Detroit begun initially by Grace Lee and Jimmy Boggs; listening to Congressman John Lewis relate his hard won knowledge of the path of struggle.[17] From witnessing their dedicated, intelligent, compassionate leadership, here are some of the things I've learned.

Motivation

People are motivated by devotion, not passion or a short-lived desire to contribute. Devotion means that, once engaged, you do not leave.

People either know or soon discover that this is the work for the rest of their lives. It will take much longer than anyone thought.

Your work occurs within history and in a specific place. It's important to locate yourself within the history of other struggles. How are you participating in and contributing to the human experience? It's also important to ground yourself in place, accepting responsibility for where you are, what has happened here, what can be learned from being here.

Action Learning

You have a theory of action. As you put that theory into action, as you interact with those in power, new strategies and practices become clear. You learn how the system works as you work with and challenge the system. You adapt to be more effective in reaching your goals.

Vigilance around behaviors and tactics is essential so that those acting to change things don't shift back to the old behaviors they're now opposing. You need to expect that the values and practices of the dominant culture will show up in you if you were raised in that system.

Time to reflect and learn from experience is essential. Knowing how to host exploratory conversations and support reflective processes are paramount leadership skills.

Thinking well, with insight and discrimination, are sources of power. Two essential skills are dialectical thinking to explore paradox, difference, and the evolution of issues; and systems thinking to determine root causes so energy is not wasted on superficial actions.

Leadership

Leaders are essential for their vision and insight. Keeping "eyes on the prize"[18] is a leadership function. But the danger for visionaries is blind followership and a cult mentality where people surrender their free will and common sense to the leader even if the leader abhors this. (And too many enjoy it.)

Leaders carefully and consciously attend to the integrity and actions of the movement: Do actions embody its values? Does it need to shift tactics and strategy? Does it need to rest and reorganize itself or seize the moment and push forward?

The work of social change requires a commitment to personal change. Leaders must be self-aware, noticing how they're being influenced and changed, in both positive and negative directions. Embodying the values is the only way to ensure their vitality.

The key to leading effectively is knowing the things that make up your environment and then helping to arrange them so that their power becomes available.

Sun Tzu, The Art of War

Grace Lee Boggs:
A Lifetime of Movement Building

Grace Lee Boggs was a lifelong activist and philosopher for social justice from 1951 to her death in 2015 at age 100. She worked with unending dedication to foster the "Next American Revolution," developing a theory of (r)evolution and putting it into practice especially in Detroit, where she worked with her husband, the activist James Boggs.[19] In the early 1970s, she wrote a piece, "Organization Means Commitment,"[20] in which she described a very different concept of revolutionary organization and leadership, developed from many long years of patient and protracted theoretical and practical struggles.

———

"We committed ourselves to transformational organizing, which does not mainly denounce and protest oppression or mobilize Americans to struggle for more material things, but challenges us as Americans to evolve or transform ourselves into more human human beings."

She defined the work of leadership with these key behaviors:

1. The organizational structure must develop every member as a leader and not depend on a few charismatic leaders.

2. Leaders of revolution, in contrast to rebellion, must make a philosophical leap and become more human human beings. In order to change/transform the world, they must change/transform themselves.

3. Leaders must learn to think dialectically, because reality is constantly changing; what is progressive at one point can turn into its opposite at a later point. And in everything there is both the positive and negative. The responsibility of revolutionary leadership in times of crisis is not just to denounce or protest oppression but to project a vision that encourages grassroots creation of positive alternatives

When asked to comment on Occupy Wall Street at its beginning in the fall of 2011, Grace thanked everyone for breaking the silence but warned them several times that they were in for a long hard struggle.[21] They needed to notice how they were part of the culture that they were opposing and, therefore, were susceptible to behaving in old ways. Most important, they needed to understand that they had the chance to create something new; therefore, they needed to be thinking about values, not just abuses.[22]

Challenges for Leaders of Social Change

As with any pattern, these behaviors are bound to occur, no matter the social cause or the individual leader. So it's wise not to take these too personally; they are unavoidable and predictable. The leader's task is to notice them and then resolve them.

- People no longer work from a commonly held identity.

- Devotion to cause becomes fundamentalist or orthodox.

- People disagree on tactics; internal opposition arises; relationships fracture.

- Dominant culture still influences people, and the new values get subsumed by the old ones.

- People take on the tactics of the opposition, especially as those intensify.

- Egotism grows as the leader receives admiration and devotion.

- The leader feels defeated by slander, misrepresentation, attacks, personal exhaustion, and despair.

- Leadership changes because of internal revolt, persecution, death, illness.

**They tried to bury us.
They didn't know we were seeds.**[23]

Q: How Do You Self-Organize an Island of Sanity?
A: You Rely on Human Human Beings

In my early years of teaching self-organizing systems to leaders, too often they thought that order for free was putting them out of a job. If they felt excited by the concept, they would often rush up to me and say, "I realize I just have to get out of the way!" If they got frightened by the prospect, they just ignored me and returned to command and control.

———

On an island of sanity, the sanity is in treating people, as Grace Lee Boggs said, as human human beings. The technical name for our species has another double descriptor: *Homo sapiens sapiens*. Seems we need the reminder.

———

Humans being human are wonderfully talented. Generally, people are internally motivated when they believe in what they're doing. We are naturally creative when we want to contribute. All people want to belong and feel part of a community. And we want our children to be safe and healthy. It is for these reasons that self-organization works so well: it engages us humans for a cause and relies on our hearts and minds to find ways forward.

And, as I already described, when humans self-organize, there is the potential for rigidity, fanaticism, and orthodoxy. When this happens, we aren't so wonderful and how we behave cannot be labeled "sane." But inside these bad behaviors, all humans still possess the same great qualities. We can trust these are present even when hidden by the veil of certainty.

———

Self-organizing requires a clear sense of identity known to everyone in the organization and the personal autonomy to figure out how to put that identity into action moment by moment.

———

There will always be differences over which actions to pursue, and that's as it should be. What's critical is that the identity is truly visible in every action. In organizations, identity is the values and principles we establish at the beginning. And then, as work gets done and decisions get made, the identity is also the culture that forms as patterns, norms, and expectations. Where there is strong agreement on who we are and sufficient trust in one another, self-organizing develops astonishing capacities and creativity. Terrorists and social justice movements each become more effective as they learn how to work with self-organization.

The first essential act for leaders of a self-organizing system is to keep watch over the identity. It is foolish to think it won't change as people make their own decisions about their actions. They will always shift it toward more extreme in order to make a difference and get attention. It is equally foolish to get so distracted by events and crises that you stop watching what's happening to the identity. If you lose focus and get absorbed in crises, you end far from where you intended to be—more controlling, more bureaucratic, less trusting, more demanding, exhausted, and wondering what happened. (I think you know this pattern. We all do.)

The second essential act of leadership is to ensure that people are using the identity to determine actions. This is especially important in a crisis when reactivity is high and there seems to be no time to reflect.

———

If you don't live by your values when things are difficult, you render them unimportant; they gradually become meaningless, and the leader gets accused of hypocrisy, a valid charge.

———

In my experience, very few leaders take advantage of order for free. They don't quite trust the power of identity to ensure coherence and continuity. As events intensify and pressures increase, control creeps in and the slippery slope takes shape. Therefore, another essential skill for leaders is self-awareness and the ability to notice who you are becoming as you respond to unending pressures. Where has fear or distrust begun to influence decisions? Where have you asserted control? Was it necessary? What happened to relationships as a result? This quality of self-reflection isn't easy, and even if you commit to it, it becomes a casualty of crises and disappears. The best way to ensure that you reflect honestly about your own behavior is to have one or more people who will speak truthfully to you. And whom you know to listen to because they have your best interest at heart.

What I've described here requires hierarchy, not a structure usually associated with self-organizing systems. Networks are self-organizing and they don't have hierarchy. But, as I've already noted, self-organization requires sane leaders.

——

Someone has to be responsible for creating coherence at the core, a dependable and trustworthy identity that people can rely on not to change too quickly.

——

Someone has to stay alert to what's happening to the identity as decisions are made and work gets done. If we're doing well, someone has to ensure that our smugness and arrogance don't seal us off from change. If we're doing badly, someone has to stop us from hunkering down and becoming overly defensive or beating ourselves up for having failed.

Even though, in my early years of promoting participation and self-organization, I was critical of leaders at the top, I've come to see that people need visionary leaders. Not charismatic demi-gods or Masters of the Universe, but people they trust because they embody the values and qualities we're working toward. Leaders don't have to be perfect, and it helps to make one's personal struggles and challenges visible. But people need to see what's possible. That it is possible to live with integrity. That humans can still live and work well together. That we can still behave as human human beings, *Homo sapiens sapiens*.

This is why we need leaders.

And why leadership can be a noble profession.

[1] The cover image for *Leadership and the New Science* is a strange attractor.

[2] If you are unfamiliar with chaos science, or want a refresher, I detail many aspects of this and other new sciences and their implications for leadership in *Leadership and the New Science* (3rd ed., 2007).

[3] For a summary of Kaufmann's work on order for free, see my coauthored book *A Simpler Way* (1996).

[4] Here are three sources I highly recommend:

Utopia Is Scary: And Other Complaints, Nicholas Carr. Brilliant article and book on how society has been changed by the Web and handheld devices. I read everything Carr writes.

A brilliant, definitive article: "I Used to Be a Human" by Andrew Sullivan, nymagazine.com, http://nymag.com/selectall/2016/09/andrew-sullivan-technology-almost-killed me.html.

"Has the Internet Become a Failed State?" by John Naughton, theguardian.com, November 27, 2016.

[5] See Sebastian Younger, *Tribes: On Homecoming and Belonging* (New York: Twelve, Hatchette Book Group, 2015).

[6] Internet "trolls" are those who use the Internet, including social media, chat rooms, forums, to intentionally harass, disturb, threaten, harm. See the next notes.

[7] Joel Stein, "How Trolls Are Ruining the Internet," *Time*, August 18, 2016.

[8] BBC Trending, http://www.bbc.com/news/blogs-trending-35111707.

[9] Ibid.

[10] In *Leadership and the New Science* (3rd ed.), Chap. 10, "The Real World"; also published in *Leader to Leader Magazine*, Summer 2006.

[11] Hassan Hassan, "Is the Islamic State Unstoppable?" nytimes.com, July 9, 2016.

[12] Harald Doornbos and Jenan Mousa. "Present at the Beginning," a series of three articles, foreignpolicy.com, August 16, 2016.

[13] Ibid.

[14] Rukmini Callimachi, "How a Secretive Branch of ISIS Built a Global Network of Killers," nytimes.com, August 3, 2016.

[15] I have to confess that you will find these ideas about self-organization in most of my books and articles until quite recently. My recognition of the critical role played by formal leaders entered my thinking in the past few years because of what I was seeing and experiencing.

[16] Tragically, the New South Africa that Mandela and others worked so hard for is besieged with difficulties, mostly social and political, and the future looks dim. See my reflections on South Africa's decline, written in 2012, in *So Far from Home*. Things have gotten much worse since then.

[17] See John Lewis's trilogy of novels done as comic books, *March,* meant to serve as a handbook for resistance. He tells the history of the civil rights movement in details that instruct and clarify the path.

[18] The title of an excellent PBS documentary on the civil rights movement, and also a phrase that appears in songs and speeches.

[19] See the work of the Boggs Center in Detroit for long-term community building from the 1960s to the present (www.boggscenter.org). In 2012, I led a Learning Journey to Detroit in partnership with the Boggs Center. We sat in a circle with Grace who was still very present and active at the age of 97. A video of her remarks to our group is here, second one down: http://margaretwheatley.com/library/videos/detroit/.

[20] "Organization Means Commitment," available as a pdf from the Boggs Center. Grace has written many fine books, including the *Next American Revolution: Sustainable Activism in the 21st Century* (Berkeley: University of California Press, 2011).

[21] Watch this inspiring short video here: https://www.youtube.com/watch?v=LvO9ooZ0vks.

[22] This widely quoted phrase has an interesting origin. The original phrase—"What didn't you do to bury me but you forgot that I was the seed"—is in a poem by Dinos Christianopoulos, a gay poet in Greece in the 1970s. A statement borne of one man's portrayal of his own marginalization by a particular society has now grown to be the rallying call of entire populations and peoples against marginalization. (Thanks, J.S.)

[23] Grace provides additional descriptors of what's required of movement builders in *Yes! Magazine,* 2005, http://www.yesmagazine.org/issues/what-makes-a-great-place/seven-great-ideas-for-movement-builders.

5. PERCEPTION

—

What You See Is All You Get

**Organisms do not experience
environments.
They create them.**

— *Richard Lewontin,* geneticist

What Science Teaches

Perception makes the world go 'round. At least this is how we perceive it. Truly, we do not know what the real world might be. We can only see it through our sense-making capacities, which include our physical senses, scientific equipment, and experiments. None of these gives us the ability to know what might be going on outside of our very limited perceptual means. Yet as humans, perceptions are all we have to answer our biggest questions: What is life's meaning? What is the Universe? Who are we as a species? The ultimate question for Western science was first asked in the early 1700s by Leibniz: "Why is there something rather than nothing?"

Even with our very limited means, understanding how we perceive has become a critical element in theories of biology, psychology, epistemology, and cosmology. If we understand both the capacities and limitations of our perceptual abilities, we might be able to learn how life came to be, how it works. And we might develop physics that can better explain the workings of the cosmos. We might even understand ourselves better and stop driving one another crazy.

Perception in Biology

Living systems are learning systems. They form and survive only as they stay actively engaged in exchanging information with their environment. Without cognition or sense making, there can be no life. In the 1970s, Humberto Maturana and Francisco Varela made a brilliant contribution to our understanding of the role of cognition in all life. "The Santiago Theory of Cognition" (they were researchers in Chile) illuminates the role of perception in living systems—plants, animals, humans.[1] The study of how living systems know and learn is now a specialized, interdisciplinary field: cognitive science.

Cognition is not a representation of an independently existing world. It is a continuous process of bringing forth a world through the process of living. We cannot see the world as a self-existing independent object—it can only be perceived through the physical senses of every species. Perception varies by species   bats use sound, dogs use hearing and smell, bees use light waves—yet the process of perception is identical. The living being chooses what to notice and then decides how it will respond to what it just chose to pay attention to. This is the essential freedom of all living beings.

As Maturana and Varela note: "You can disturb a living system; you can never direct it." You can't boss life around unless you force it to become lifeless.

As a living system decides what to notice from the unlimited stimuli in its environment, it shapes the environment into its own little world. "It brings forth a world,"[2] through what it chooses to notice. It doesn't matter what exists beyond the perceptual filters of the organism. By its choices, it determines what's relevant and what's not. Everything else disappears.

The freedom to decide what to notice and how to respond has a fundamental impact on the environment. It changes it. The environment that the organism creates becomes its means of support for continuing to live. Or not. If it shapes it, as we humans have done, in narrow, life-destroying ways, eventually the environment fails and so too does the species.

Perception in Physics

The thought experiment known as Schrödinger's Cat was designed by Erwin Schrödinger to put an end to the "central mystery" of quantum physics.[3] His experiment was meant to refute the double-slit experiment in which the behavior of electrons, either as waves or particles, depended on the experiment and the expectations of a human observer. The electrons changed their behavior according to what the observer was looking for. In his thought experiment, the cat was in a closed box and its fate was determined by the observer. Even though Schrödinger had expected to disprove such an absurdity, this experiment only substantiated this fundamental weirdness. Years later, Schrödinger opined, "I wish I'd never met the cat."

The first evidence that perception made a difference in observed behaviors of light appeared more than 300 years ago, in the 1790s in the work of Thomas Young. Experimentation continued and, up until 1925, there was no satisfactory theory of quantum mechanics. And then, by the end of 1926, there were two, each different from the other.[4] Since then, the double-slit experiment has continued to perplex, disturb, depress, and stimulate quantum theorists. They can calculate using very different theories and each still get useful results. The Nobel Prize for Physics was awarded first to a father, then later to his son, for their research that gave opposite explanations, both of which were right.[5]

Very recently (2013), researchers in Japan and Italy announced the results of what is the definitive double-slit experiment, where they observed the behavior of single electrons. Using a membrane with slits that were each 62 nanometers wide (a nanometer is a billionth of a meter), they observed the behavior of electrons as they passed through the slits when both were open or when only one was open. The patterns made it clear that the electrons were acting as both waves and particles, the same as in past experiments. "Each electron seemed to 'know' not only what the exact experimental set-up was at the time it flew through the slit, but also what had happened to the electrons that went before it and the ones that would come after it."[b]

Richard Feynman, the preeminent American physicist, said that the double-slit experiment contains "the central mystery, indeed the only mystery" of quantum mechanics. It has remained so to this day. It might be demonstrating a different role for perception; it might be demonstrating the limits of physics as currently understood; it might be pointing to the deeper mystery of how all is interconnected.

And nobody knows how the world can be like that.[7]

I think I can safely say that nobody understands quantum mechanics. . . . Do not keep saying to yourself, if you can possibly avoid it, "But how can it be like that?" Nobody knows how it can be like that.

Richard Feynman, physicist

The Blinders of Inexplicable Arrogance

Scientists, based on their own experiments, have come face-to-face with great mystery. Modern scientific ways of understanding the Universe are proving insufficient to explain observable phenomena. While humility would seem to be the natural response, this encounter with not knowing has led to a heightened sense of ego among those who believe that modern science is the only valid lens. They propose that science is what makes us special; perhaps we are a uniquely talented species only existing on Earth. In the face of so much uncertainty, claiming this specialness seems strange. And it places frightening blinders on our perceptions.

Scientists have increased their perceptual abilities with new technologies, but even these advances reveal only infinitesimally small bits of information relative to the unfathomable dimensions of the Universe. New telescopes, space probes, and computational methods are revealing a cosmos whose dimensions approach infinity—true cause for wonder. In the face of these astonishing discoveries, instead of wonder and humility, most scientists hang onto their traditional ways of understanding, known as scientific materialism. The world can be understood in terms of current physical laws of time, space, energy, and matter. These laws are being challenged by increasing evidence from their own experiments, as you will read here. But in order to hold onto the existing paradigm, theoretical physicists are proposing outrageously fanciful theories, none of which meet a primary rule of science, that hypotheses be testable.

I am not condemning science nor devaluing its superb contribution to our understanding of how life works. I wouldn't be writing this book based on scientific understandings if I felt that way. What I am speaking out against is the common practice among scientists to condemn and exclude other ways of knowing at this time when science itself is in a deep struggle to understand how this Universe works.[8]

———

There are other ways of knowing reality, reliable methods that have served humans and earlier hominids for millennia. It is the arrogance of our science that denies their existence and their usefulness.

———

Years ago, I realized that in all human cultures—all of them—there were ways of knowing beyond the five senses that supported their survival and manifested in their cultural expressions and rituals. They knew there is more going on than what our five human senses reveal, and usually they named other senses, such as intuition and consciousness. They had detailed maps and complex practices that enabled them to work with the order inherent in the world.

I am not speaking of spiritual beliefs. I am noting that human cultures have developed their own sciences for interacting with the elements, the planet and the Universe. Western science dismisses this vast body of human wisdom by labeling it magic, ignorance, or science illiteracy. But our science is just the most recent means to make sense of reality. Its arrogance is neither justified nor helpful.

PERCEPTION: FACING REALITY

It is in our nature to ask questions of existence. And also predictably, as soon as we discover what appears to be an answer, it becomes orthodoxy, the only belief system tolerated. Too many scientists now believe that their answers are the one true answer. And their answer to everything observed is materialism. If phenomena can't be explained by physical manifestations, they don't exist. If we can't locate a function such as intuition or consciousness in the brain, it doesn't exist. But the most troubling consequence of materialist thinking is this: If it is found to exist in the brain, if the brain can be stimulated to create that experience, then it only exists in the brain. Once physical evidence exists, scientists conclude that everything comes from brain activity—there is no reality beyond the physical.[9] This is perhaps the greatest threat from neuroscience, the reduction of the numinous and mysterious to a specific site in the brain, thereby denying any other reality.[10]

This reductionism denies the experience of those who claim other ways of knowing and working with reality, myself included. I have benefitted immeasurably from working with the worldview of Tibetan Buddhism and from the wisdom traditions of many indigenous peoples. In 2014, I wrote *How Does Raven Know?* to introduce people to a world of forgotten companions, known in all wisdom traditions.[11] Whenever I read a scientist who mocks things like intuition or who wants to educate us poor deluded ones, I either feel angry or sad. (Sad is the more compassionate reaction, of course.) How lonely it must feel to shrink the world into five meager senses that can perceive only 1–2 percent of the light spectrum.

What hasn't shrunk is a giant ego expression known as the Anthropic Principle. One aspect of this theory postulates that the Universe has created us as conscious beings because it needed a way to reflect back on itself. Let's think about this for a moment.

In 2016, using new computational methods and new telescopes, the number of probable galaxies rose from 200 billion to 2 trillion, each of which would contain 100 billion stars.[12]

———

We humans live on a medium-size planet rotating around an average-size star. And we're the ones that the Universe has tasked with consciousness? (Comedian George Carlin believes the Universe created humans so it could have plastic.[13])

I think I can understand the source of such arrogance (some days I can; some days I can't). It comes from the fear that our ability to comprehend the Universe is failing us. This is what made Einstein fearful: if separated particles, no matter how distant they are from each other, act as one inseparable unit, this would make the Universe incomprehensible. And it does, as you'll read in Section Six, Interconnectedness.

As a paradigm exhausts its sense-making capacities, people always grasp onto it more desperately, insisting that it still works, that it can and will answer all questions. As physicists search to understand their experiments, they are trapped inside their paradigm. They can only seek physical explanations no matter how crazy these are. There is a distinction between theoretical and applied physics. Applied physicists don't understand why things work, but they make things that work. They keep producing new technologies from which we benefit (for now). It is theoretical physics that is facing the great questions—the existence of space, the meaning of time, questions of infinity. As they struggle to understand the quantum world—of a participative Universe in which particles seem to know what has happened before and what will happen next—they have gotten lost in conjectures that are so incredulous to contemplate that "weird " does not begin to describe them.[14]

———

Here's one of my favorite quotes from the physicist Wolfgang Pauli as he judged a theory: "This is so bad it's not even wrong."

———

This phrase has been used to describe the current state of cosmological thinking in physics. Roger Penrose, one of the great physicists of our time, has recanted some of his earlier fancies in a new book, *Fashion, Faith, and Fantasy in the New Physics of the Universe*. He states that most of the current fantastical ideas about the origins of the Universe cannot be true (possibly including the Big Bang) but that an even wilder reality may lie behind them.

I'm not disturbed by what theoretical physicists are dreaming up; I'm content to let them get lost in their mathematics and imaginings to explain action-at-a-distance. But what feels important to me is to call out how they discredit all other forms of knowing, which harms all of us as we try to understand this world.

———

Let's not dismiss the hundreds of thousands of years of human wisdom that gave the capacity to create, decorate, and know a world far richer in powers and capacities than materialistic science can ever fathom.

If we want to understand who humans have been, including earlier hominids that predate our species, there is stunning evidence from archeology. We and our early ancestors have been far more creative, caring, and knowing than any neuroscience can ever explain.[15]

- The first evidence of a stone implement carved, never used, and offered as a gift in burial, is 300,000 years old. It is a very beautiful object of two-colored rose quartz, material transported from 75 miles away. Thirty-two bodies were carefully buried at this site.[16]

- Flutes tuned to the pentatonic scale (the most common scale among humans) were skillfully carved from the wing bones of birds 40,000 years ago. These flutes can still be played today.[17]

- The Chauvet cave paintings in France are about 32,000 years old. They have a level of artistry not seen again until the Italian Renaissance. They painted in this sophisticated way continuously for 22,000 years.

- Bone necklaces worn in both northern and southern Africa date from 100,000 years ago. It is assumed such objects indicate social stratification or clans.

How hominids have created culture and community for at least half a million years is purely wondrous. Our most favored explanatory lens, scientific materialism, cannot begin to explain what's been going on here for hundreds of thousands of years. To reduce all these manifestations to crass survival strategies is ridiculous. To believe that we have now achieved superior status from our ancestors is worth questioning.

Our perceptions of who we are and what we are capable of need to be expanded, not contracted into demeaning or fanciful explanations. We need to know far more about our species and this Universe we inhabit. We cannot afford the luxury of arrogance that denies other ways of knowing.

———

I began studying prehistory and anthropology a few years ago, at the same time that I was studying the patterns of collapse of civilizations. As I spent more time reading about what was going on here so very long ago, I realized that anthropology had become my escape literature. It was a wonderful way to shift my attention from all the painful things I was observing daily.

And yet, over these years I've come to realize that my familiarity with what has gone before gives me a strange comfort. Standing in the past, honoring the wonder and not-knowing, acknowledging early ancestors— all this has led to my deepening commitment to make this *Now* as meaningful as possible.

Why not? What have we got to lose?

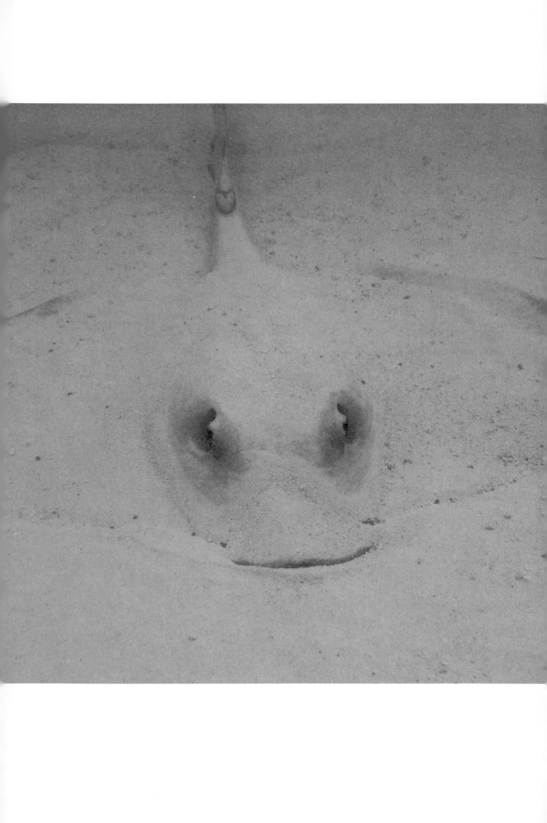

Other Ways of Knowing

all living beings through all time
have needed to know the world well
knowing life depends on this

most peoples throughout time
have seen beyond the visible world
they and still we rely on
symbols objects rituals
to summon forces of protection and plenty
knowing to respect and evoke
the unseen world with offerings

modern culture is an anomaly
to the pattern of human cultures
withdrawing from everything
except our five material senses

arrogant with vision that sees
about 1% of what
the light spectrum reveals

seeing so little we grow more
frantic to know what is out there
yet push aside those who see

no wonder we are fearful of
being harmed as we harm the world
scared humans scarring sacred world

Margaret Wheatley, How Does Raven Know?

Cognitive Dissonance

My doctoral dissertation, written in 1978, used cognitive dissonance to understand behaviors in a bank's corporate team tasked with creating new training programs. We were looking at the same information, but everyone was using it to fortify different positions. We had gathered the information from face-to-face interviews, in-person observations of programs, student comments, and final evaluations. I don't recall that we used any numeric measurements as there was more to choose from at that time: numbers were not as deified as they are now. I might call this the era of quality measures, as they're now known. I take pleasure in even thinking about these good old days.

Once we had all the information, the team would sit and analyze it together—sometimes this would take a few days. Then we would put recommendations in a final report (on paper) and present it up the hierarchy for decisions and funding. Today we speak about "slow" leadership, slow food, slow lifestyles. Those of us working before twenty-first-century cyber-speed took hold know what the concept of slow means. It worked well—we had time to collect good information, to think it through together and enjoy working together as a team. Sigh.

I used cognitive dissonance in my dissertation to understand what, at that time, felt strange. There we were, looking at the same information whose conclusions felt obvious to me, and each person was coming up with very different, even opposing conclusions. I was young—I still believed in rational analyses, so their behavior was a surprise. But not now. Cognitive dissonance is the norm, visible everywhere, and I no longer expect to see rational behavior employed in decision making. However, I still expect it at home and with my own colleagues.

Cognitive dissonance is a well-established theory of human cognition. Each person has sense-making patterns of how things work, developed over time from experiences, acculturation, and other developmental influences. Our view of how the world works gets patterned into our brains as physical neuronal pathways. These habitual responses act as filters for information.

———

Habits save time: it's easier to do the same thing, or think the same thing. Changing our minds takes attention and work.

———

And we couldn't get through a day if every situation was treated as new. However, when we are looking at information that could be important, dismissing it as familiar or responding habitually to it can be dangerous. Instead of seeing what's new, we see the new through old eyes. And this gets us into trouble.

Even those skilled in the scientific method run into this perceptual problem. In his truly seminal book *The Structure of Scientific Revolutions*, Thomas Kuhn woke us up to the power of paradigms or worldviews that shape perception. He observed that scientists (even scientists) would behave as we all do when confronted with data that contradicted their working hypothesis. Either they would see only those pieces of data that confirmed their hypothesis, or they would twist their interpretation of the data so it was confirming or, in the extreme case, they would look at the data and physically not see it.[18]

To give credit to scientists, at least they have a working hypothesis that they're testing. Most of us have no idea of the assumptions and beliefs we use to create our perceptions. We think we're open-minded and curious when, in fact, we all suffer from "paradigm blindness."[19] This is the perennial problem with human perception that can only be solved through awareness. The nineteenth-century philosopher William James said, "As a rule, we disbelieve all theories and facts for which we have no use."

Cognitive dissonance explains this phenomenon; it offers both a diagnosis and a remedy. First, we have to acknowledge that we're all wearing blinders, every single one of us. Everyone has their view of reality, and it will always be dismally incomplete. Yet whatever the view, it's essential to note that some views are more accurate and/or helpful than others, as they're based on more information or life-affirming values. I have no patience with the prevalent attitude that "It's all just story." What might sound like acceptance or tolerance is much more likely to be dismissal. Or laziness. Not all stories are equal in their content nor their consequences. We need to look carefully at what happens with a story as it moves in the world; people need to be held accountable for what they put out there, especially in this "post-truth" era.

We do not see the world as an objective, self-existing reality. We can't. Nobody can, even with advanced scientific equipment. We will never know if such a reality exists. What we do know is that the human brain processes information through a strong filter that has been unconsciously and consciously created as the means to interact with the external environment.

Everything alive has cognition and uses it to determine what to notice. We humans, with higher mental powers, complexify the process of cognition. We see the world through a well-constructed, tightly controlled personality. This is not a good thing: It reduces our cognitive capacity. Instead of being conscious, we are *self*-conscious. And this leads, as I've already noted, to our opinionated, popularity-seeking, narcissistic, self-protecting, fundamentalist, paranoid culture.

This would be bad enough if it was only a problem for individuals trying to make sense of an overly stimulating, confusing world. Increasingly cognitive dissonance is in politics, bringing a vicious intensity to debates, making it impossible to use reason to address our biggest problems. The rise of hate-driven right-wing political parties, even in formerly reasonable countries,[20] and the increase in incendiary rhetoric from all sides, is evidence of how cognitive dissonance has replaced rational behavior.[21]

How is it, in the face of recurring natural disasters, that climate change still seems to be invisible—except to those affected by the most recent floods, fires, cyclones? How can so much evidence and direct experience of climate change remain invisible? Because of the power of human perception.

Cognitive Dissonance and Weapons of Mass Destruction (WMDs)

In July 2016, a comprehensive report was issued about Britain's decision to join the United States in war against Iraq. Tony Blair was Britain's prime minister. The Chilcot report, named after the chairman of the inquiry, Sir John Chilcot, is a damning description of poor and hasty decision making, blunt ego posturing, and retrospective justification for decisions.[22] All of these are common in leadership, but the consequences are the world we now live in: over 100,000 Iraqi civilians killed, more displaced as refugees, the rise of ISIS and global terrorism, and the wars now raging in the Middle East including Iraq, those wars driving millions to flee and creating Europe's refugee crisis.

This report holds Blair publicly accountable for his actions. But let's not delude ourselves into thinking that other leaders, upon reading this report, will learn from this and proceed more cautiously in responding to threats, real and perceived.

———

Blair's justifications are a tragic study in cognitive dissonance. In the lead-up to war, he maintains his position, continually asserting that there were weapons of mass destruction in Iraq even when, as evidence mounted, they did not exist.[23]

———

In late September 2002, before the war, he made a speech where he emphatically stated, "His [Saddam Hussein's] WMD program is active, detailed and growing. . . . He has existing plans for the use of weapons, which could be activated in 45 minutes."

When no evidence of WMDs was forthcoming, Blair reframed this. They certainly existed—they just hadn't been found yet. He shifted the discovery of WMDs into the future in a later speech in 2003 to the House of Commons: "There are literally thousands of sites . . . but it is only now that the Iraq Survey Group has been put together that a dedicated team of people . . . will be able to do the job properly. . . . I have no doubt that they will find the clearest possible evidence of WMD."

Twelve months later, when the Iraq Survey Group still hadn't found the weapons, Blair still couldn't accept that WMDs were not there. Instead, he changed tack again, arguing in a speech that "they could have been removed, they could have been hidden, they could have been destroyed."

When this stance became untenable because there were no WMDs, Blair reached for a new justification for the war: "I can apologize for the information that turned out to be wrong, but I can't, sincerely at least, apologize for removing Saddam. The world is a better place with Saddam in prison."

Conspiracy Theories

On December 14, 2012, in Newtown, Connecticut, twenty young children and seven adults were killed at the Sandy Hook elementary school by a twenty-year-old young man using an automatic weapon (he had killed his mother on his way to the massacre).

I have been aware of the insane number of conspiracy theories that circulate online about everything. I've watched some of them in mocking disbelief, and I've enjoyed comedians who make fun of them. But I was ignorant of the conspiracy theories that began circulating immediately after the Sandy Hook slaying of the innocents. For all that is being written about Internet hatred and trolls,[24] I am still stunned by what the community of Newtown has had to endure because of the conspiracy theorists who seized on this tragedy and did not cease in their manic pursuits for any bits of information that would confirm their insanity.

———

The father of a slain six-year-old reported that many people didn't believe his son had died or even that he had lived at all.

———

Days after the rampage, a man walked around Newtown filming a video in which he declared that the massacre had been staged by "some sort of New World Order global elitists" intent on taking away our guns and our liberty. A week later, James Tracy, a professor at Florida Atlantic University, wrote a blog post expressing doubts about the massacre. By January, a 30-minute YouTube video, titled "The Sandy Hook Shooting—

Fully Exposed," which asked questions like "Wouldn't frantic kids be a difficult target to hit?" had been viewed more than 10 million times."[25]

You are aware (how could you not be) of many long-standing conspiracy theories: The Holocaust never happened; we never landed on the Moon. Fourteen European countries have laws making Holocaust denial a criminal offense.[26] But the Internet is a lawless realm. Fear and hatred motivate people to spend hours going over videos and photos to find tiny clues that substantiate their conspiracy theories. These clues that seem so obvious to them are woven together in a coherent story; this storyline is then used in endless confrontations with officials (who are assumed to be part of the conspiracy).

———

They aren't looking for the truth—although they call themselves "truthers." They are looking for confirmation of what they have chosen to fear.

———

Once the theory is set in motion, it is immutable to change. If evidence is presented from an outside source that might disconfirm it, such information is not denied. It is twisted into further evidence in support of the conspiracy. Perceptual filters take anything presented and warp it into confirming evidence.

This is the power of perception run amok. Polished by fear into an obscuring, microscopic lens, what becomes visible under scrutiny can only look the same. In their hermetically sealed bunkers of the mind, change is not a possibility.

The father of the slain six-year-old first spent years trying to give accurate information, even getting involved in a four-hour online exchange with the conspiracy theorists (some asked for proof that he was the real father; others demanded that his son's body be exhumed.) These strategies led nowhere and caused him to go on the offensive using legal means to take down websites, stop their funding efforts, getting Tracy, the professor, fired, and removing hundreds of photos of his son by legal means, invoking copyright laws. But at enormous emotional and physical cost to himself—he has moved five times to avoid being found, including after the release of this article about him.

Other members of the Newtown community have also gone on the offensive because, as the father said, "People don't understand what trolls are," he said. "If you don't feed them, they don't just go away." Another group has used the tactics of trolls, sending threatening emails to the family members of the main hoaxers and, bizarrely, sending them rubber ducks in the mail, which the hoaxers immediately assume are poisonous.[27]

What a horrible and obscene story this is. Yet it reveals so much about this time and the descent into hatred and self-protection.

We need to see this clearly. The enemies are not only outside the gates. They are here inside, haters unleashing deadly vehemence against innocent victims, using the very same technology that was meant to open us to the world and bring us together.

Depending on Diversity

When a paradigm no longer provides reliable guidance for how to live in the world, the most common response is to grasp hold of it more firmly. As it dawns on us that we don't know how things work—that it's not working—we become more insistent that it has to work just as we thought it did. Opening to the uncertainty, to the need for a new way of seeing, is not what we humans do well. We use our big brains and our powers of cognition to resist change. Our skills at manipulating information lead us to become more fundamentalist, more certain.

We see this type of fundamentalism in too many leaders these days as they grasp for handholds in practices that didn't work in the past, but that they robotically keep doing, as if they have no choice. It didn't work before, but at least they know how to do it that way, so let's do it again. For a while, this repetitive behavior offers the comfort that actions are being taken, but it is also Einstein's familiar definition of stupidity—doing the same thing twice and expecting different results.

At some point, leaders realize it's just not working. Often it takes a major crisis to wake people up. But we can be smarter than that. The crises are already here. If we're willing to notice our own pursuit of certainty, to see that our favored ways of working aren't working, then we can use these magnificent powers of perception to obtain a clearer sense of reality.

———

Can certainty give way to curiosity?
Can arrogance give way to humility?
If so, we may be able to perceive what the environment has been trying to tell us all along.

In the After Action Review (AAR) process (see p. 128), its core strength is the profound respect for different perceptions. It is acknowledged from the start that everyone who was involved in the situation under review saw something that others probably missed. Or they saw things that only they could have noticed because of where they were at the time and who they are in the ranks. I was told that it took about fifteen years for soldiers to be able to speak truthfully in the presence of senior commanders. And it took even longer for senior commanders to appreciate the perspectives of those below them. What motivated everyone to learn how to think well together was the shared imperative of learning. It's better to learn than be dead.

As often as I've repeated that phrase to leaders, I knew they couldn't experience it with the same force as did the military. And of course this would be true. But now it's not. We no longer can afford the luxury of certainty or arrogance. If we're going to resist the life-destroying dynamics at play, we have to become as serious about learning as were those tired, hungry young soldiers standing at the back of a dusty truck.

We need to depend on diversity. It's not about respecting difference for ethical reasons. It's recognizing that none of us can ever see the situation clearly enough to act well on our own. Working with diversity is a life-saving capacity as well as an honoring of one another.

———

Diversity is valuing difference because it makes a difference: We see more when there are more of us seeing. We know more when everyone's perspective is sought and incorporated into our learning.

Participative processes, listening skills, conflict resolution, problem-solving skills—these need to be in every leader's repertoire. Over the past several decades, many excellent processes have been developed and tested in the heat of controversy. Resources are plentiful, and I expect that you've already used them on numerous occasions.[28]

What I want to ask you is how often you use them *now*. All of these processes, including the AAR, require that scarcest of resources, time. Some processes take hours; some serve up good results only when given days.

They all require that we take time: to think, to settle in, to calm down, to sit still, to listen quietly, to not react instantly, to not pull out our phones, to not get distracted, to not get impatient, to . . . .

It is evident that these processes demand behaviors completely counter to our present ones. Some might call these *revolutionary* processes because they're so foreign in our workplaces and homes. I choose to call them *restorative*. They are processes that reawaken our powers of cognition, reinstitute thinking, and redirect our attention to one another. The unintended but predictable outcome of these is that people once again feel confident and smart. We learn how to make sense of what formerly overwhelmed us, not only because we've opened our own minds but, as a collective of minds, we see more clearly. And the phrase "We're all in this together" takes on real meaning.

The leader's task is to ensure that thinking together is just the way we do our work. Learning is our highest priority. Once embedded in the culture, there is no question that you will have restored the means for people to act with those extraordinary powers attributed to our species when we labeled ourselves *Homo sapiens sapiens*.

A Tale of Two Stories

One of the key lenses into an organization's leadership and culture is how it deals with crises. What happens when something goes wrong or the leaders feel under attack? In these moments, the organization's real values become startlingly visible. Do leaders panic and scramble to get out of a tough situation, forgetting principles and values? Or do they take the time to work with the crisis, engaging their members fully, relying on their history, values, and principles—that is, their identity? Only in the latter case is it possible to create the strong social fabric that enables an institution to move confidently into its desired future.

I want to share with you two stories that helped me understand an important role for leaders when a crisis arises. They both are strong examples of how to work well with life's dynamics of identity, self-organization, and perception. In both cases, I wasn't aware of this critical leadership role of actively dealing with perceptions until I heard the stories.

The Gift and The Firestorm

I observed the behavior described here in real time while I was working with the president of the Illinois Math and Science Academy (IMSA), Dr. Stephanie Pace Marshall. Stephanie was the founding president for the country's first three-year residential school for students talented in science and math. Founded in 1985, long before STEM (science, technology, engineering, math) became the top priority for schools, I watched up close as these educators, working in a self-organizing environment, pioneered many educational innovations that have since become common practice: problem-based learning; inquiry-based science; integrated science. Stephanie, like all the wise leaders I know, worked from a clear theory of action. She knew not only what to do but why to do it.[29]

And she kept developing that theory in her day-to-day leadership. She became a clear guiding voice for how to create educational environments that generate learning and motivation in all children. Her consistent vision has been to liberate the goodness and genius of all children, for the world. She has supported thousands of educators to create life-affirming, generative learning environments.

In August of one year, the head of admissions came to her with a terrible error—they had mistakenly admitted thirty-two children who were on the waiting list. The director wanted to immediately write to them and tell them their acceptance had been a mistake, but Stephanie would have none of that. Referencing their values and vision, she declared that they would figure out how to welcome these new students, even though they had no idea of where they'd get everything they needed in one month, from residential mattresses to faculty to counselors to computers.

Faced with so much uncertainty, the staff erupted with very strong emotions. Stephanie was aware of the atmosphere of angst-filled emotions. She felt she needed to learn more about their underlying stories, what lay beneath these strong emotions. To do so, she sent one colleague to listen in on the conversations going on at lunch and the faculty room. She wanted to know what people were saying in detail and what role they were in (but no names). When the assigned eavesdropper returned with pages of quotes, Stephanie read through them very slowly, gaining perspective at the 30,000-foot level.

Two very clear stories emerged, which she labeled The Gift and The Firestorm. The Gift story was one of welcome, of grateful parents, of people feeling proud to have figured out how to welcome in the unexpected students. The Firestorm was filled with blame toward Stephanie for having made a decision to accept the extra students, recounting a litany of her past bad behaviors, even threatening to unionize.

At her opening talk in September, she displayed symbols of the two stories, a wrapped gift box and a fire. Each image was arrayed with the direct quotes of staff and faculty. "Usually we don't know the competing stories and we just keep doing what we've been doing, locked into the familiar narrative. Now you see two. It's time for you to choose."

Since this event many years ago, Stephanie has taught many leaders to focus on discerning the stories their organizations are living, usually unconsciously. The power for change comes from identifying the narrative and, as a collective, consciously choosing the one they want to live into. It's not strategic plans, she says, that create change. We need to see clearly the narrative we are blindly following and consciously choose the storyline of who we want to become.[30]

If Stephanie had not named the stories, or if a strong sense of identity had not been present, the negativity would have continued and the staff would have divided into two factions. Instead, they willingly supported the story that exemplified their identity and aspirations. New students were welcomed in and it all worked out well. Thereafter, staff used the two symbols as shorthand to notice their behaviors. As they were making decisions or determining actions, they would ask each other: Are we acting from Firestorm or Gift? They knew which story they wanted to make true.

Leadership Lessons from Besieged Nuns

The strongest women leaders on the planet today are nuns. I've worked with a wide diversity of leaders on all continents for over forty years, and nowhere have I found better leadership than among women religious.

They know whom they serve and are consistently creative in finding ways to meet the needs of the poor, the downtrodden, the marginalized. After years of working with them in a befriending, consultative role, I coined the slogan "If you want it done, ask a nun."

And then, in 2009, instead of serving those living at the margins, they became the marginalized when the Vatican determined that American women religious needed to be investigated because they had become too secularized, too feminist, too radical. (This was the first of two Vatican impositions. You've already read how the formal leaders of all nuns handled demands for obedience; see p. 92. What I describe here was an earlier investigation conducted on all U.S. nuns and sisters, and what I learned from one congregation's powerful way to deal with this investigation.)

In late 2009, the Vatican mandated an Apostolic Visitation to "look into the quality of the life" of apostolic institutes of women religious in the United States. Over a period of two years, nearly 100 of the 400 institutes (how the sisters organize) were paid actual visits by Vatican designated observers. (All 400 had to complete documentation.) Whatever the stated purpose was, it appeared that this was part of the Vatican's efforts to control the behavior of American sisters. The Vatican's public statements were very harsh, disrespectful, critical, filled with misunderstandings and factual errors. Many sisters, especially the older ones at the end of more than fifty years of consecrated service, felt deep grief and anger. Yet even with these strong emotions present, they relied on their history, charisms, and communities to find their way through, very unusual behavior in any beleaguered or threatened group.

PERCEPTION: RESTORING SANITY

Women religious are well trained in how to discern, to think, and to achieve true consensus. They have long years of experience with reflection, contemplation, and prayer. When they make a decision, everyone has participated in the process, and they are united in how to move forward. The visitation process challenged them deeply; in the midst of fear and doubt, consensus seemed a distant goal. Yet each religious order had to decide on how their institutes or chapters would deal with the visitors.

The story I'm relaying here came from my work with the Sisters of St. Joseph (the U.S. Federation organized into sixteen congregations). Let me pause here to tell you the firm foundation they stand on, a history that always moves me to tears.

Founded in 1650 in France, the Sisters of St. Joseph began as a noncloistered order for ordinary women to be able to work in their communities with "the dear neighbor." With the political turmoil of the impending French Revolution, they disbanded and went into hiding. Four of their leaders were condemned to the guillotine, and three were beheaded in one afternoon. But then it grew too dark to continue. The remaining sister, Jeanne Fontbonne, was returned to her cell to await execution the next day. But that night, the French Revolution began with the overthrow of Robespierre, and the executioners were deposed. Jeanne went on to refound the order, which was soon filled with sisters.

In 1836, six sisters ventured to St. Louis to teach deaf children. They had been asked to come to the wild New World by a French bishop who had been advised by a friend to "get the Sisters of St. Joseph because they will do anything."[31]

This was their history, which they all knew in detail, as they prepared for the Vatican investigations in 2010. At their federation meetings, they debated many approaches, and none were acceptable to all. These were well-tempered conversations, but the distress was also palpable: Why were they investigating us? How should we respond?

And then it all came together. I don't recall whether it was one of their leaders or an outside advisor, but someone read aloud the Vatican's statements on domestic abuse. In the silence of that room, the sisters contemplated whether they were the victims of such abuse from priests in power in the Vatican, abuse as defined by the Vatican. Through more conversations and contemplation, they reached a shared understanding that this was an accurate albeit difficult description: they were experiencing domestic abuse.

What happened next shows the incredible power of a shared story. Once they agreed on a shared definition of the problem, they could trust one another as to how best to handle it in their separate congregations.

Collectively, they named the pattern of behaviors they were encountering. As individual congregations, they could be trusted to respond appropriately.

In each of these stories, the role of shared perception is clearly evident. If we are grounded in a common story, one that we choose together, and if we trust one another, then we each are free to use this shared story to make individual decisions. Whatever the particular story might be, it will have resonance only if it is grounded in a shared identity that includes our history and aspirations for who we want to be. Within that identity, a story serves to create a sharper focus to our perceptions; collectively, we interpret the present situation in the same way.

This is a critical leadership responsibility as the organization moves through crises and even in calm times (if these even exist now). It is the leader's role to make visible the stories, usually unconscious, that people are acting from. And then to consciously name a more empowering story linked to the identity. There are many images for the role that a shared story plays in self-organizing: it is a shared perceptual filter; it creates coherence at the core; it is the reference point for individual actions; it is an aspiration of who we choose to be.

The results are most often astonishing. People feel empowered to make their own decisions, held by colleagues in an atmosphere of trust and encouragement. This atmosphere gives rise to individual and collective confidence. The heavy, dark energy of the challenges lightens as people engage willingly in what needs to get done. And once through a difficult time, people emerge with a stronger sense of belonging, with both the confidence and competence that they can handle whatever is next.

———

Life offers us this great gift of self-organization, how we can be held in the basin of shared meaning and, within that, exercise individual freedom. It is such a shame to waste it on fear and doubt. Or to seek to contain and control it.

PERCEPTION: NOTES

[1] *The Systems View of Life*, p. 252. Well worth reading is the original book, *The Tree of Knowledge: The Biological Roots of Human Understanding*, by Humberto Maturana and Francisco Varela (Boston: Shambhala Publications, 1987). When I first read this book, my world view shifted suddenly and quite wonderfully.

[2] Ibid., p. 256.

[3] Read more about this and its implications for leadership in *Leadership and the New Science* (3rd ed.), Chap. 4.

[4] Gribbin, *The Quantum Mystery*, Kindle locations 394–395.

[5] J. J. Thomson received the Nobel Prize in 1906 for proving that electrons are particles. He lived to see his son, George Thomson, receive the Nobel Prize in 1937 for proving that electrons are waves. Both of them were right; both awards were justified. In Gribbin, Kindle location 350.

[6] Gribbin, Kindle locations 554–555.

[7] If you're intrigued by the central mystery and its development over time, John Gribbin's short book is very useful. He ends the book with this statement.

[8] Deepak Chopra does the math for how much of the Universe is observable through Western science: 70 percent is Dark Energy and 26 percent is Dark Matter, neither of which we understand or can observe. Of the remaining 4 percent that we do observe, nearly all of that is invisible. He concludes that our present science can only speak to 0.01 percent of what's going on.

I recommend watching this Deepak Chopra presentation at the Science and NonDuality Conference, late 2016, for an excellent explanation of how the Universe is consciousness or awareness. His thesis is in complete concordance with great spiritual traditions. "The Final Destination: The Human Universe," at https://www.youtube.com/watch?v=dgPVhe56hT8. This is drawn from his new book, *You Are the Universe*.

[9] Here's an article on dreams with a subtitle that diminishes sacred experiences to neuroscience's explanation of how revelations happen in the brain: https://aeon.co/essays/why-are-dreams-such-potent-vehicles-for-the-supernatural?

[10] In the Mind and Life dialogues with neuroscientists, the Dalai Lama insists on the distinction between the brain and Mind. These dialogues can be seen on his website.

[11] *How Does Raven Know? Entering Sacred World: A Meditative Memoir*. Note: this book is only available for purchase on my website: http://margaretwheatley.com/books-products/books/raven-know/.

[12] http://www.skyandtelescope.com/astronomy-news/universe-2-trillion-galaxies/.

[13] Watch Carlin's brilliant video on human arrogance: https://www.youtube.com/watch?v=2cjRGee5ipM.

[14] Gribbin details four attempts to explain nonlocality. Words fail me as I read these.

[15] Photos and more descriptions are in my book *How Does Raven Know?*

[16] *Becoming Human: Innovation in Prehistoric Material and Spiritual Culture*, ed. Colin Renfrew and Iain Morley (Cambridge: Cambridge University Press, 2009), p. 18.

[17] Listen to one of these flutes in Werner Herzog's dramatic and arresting movie about the Chauvet caves: *The Cave of Forgotten Dreams*. It's a very eerie experience.

[18] Thomas Kuhn's book was published in 1962. It introduced us to paradigm change and was itself a paradigm changer for science, social science, and philosophy. Kuhn has been very important to my own work.

[19] Joel Barker's term. I still greatly value his work of bringing an awareness of paradigms into business; "The Business of Paradigms" was a video I used many times. And I've used his quote, "What is difficult to solve with one paradigm becomes easy to solve with another," as a guiding principle for my work of attempting to shift the paradigm of leadership.

[20] As in Denmark where, in World War II, many people wore yellow stars to protect Jews from the Nazis. http://www.nytimes.com/2016/09/06/world/europe/denmark-migrants-refugees-racism.html.

[21] "Chilcot: Why We Cover Our Ears to the Facts," http://www.bbc.com/news/magazine-36744911.

[22] See an assessment of the Chilcot Report's major conclusions here: https://www.theguardian.com/uk-news/2016/jul/06/iraq-inquiry-key-points-from-the-chilcot-report.

[23] All quotes from "Chilcot: Why We Cover Our Ears to the Facts," http://www.bbc.com/news/magazine-36744911.

[24] See this handbook for dealing with hate directed at you: Danielle Keats Citron, *Hate Crimes in Cyberspace* (Cambridge, MA: Harvard University Press, 2014).

[25] This father has spent years fighting back against the "hoaxers," trying a variety of strategies that have somewhat succeeded. The article is worth reading for the details of the activities of conspiracy theorists and what pushbacks and legal maneuvers seem to stop them or make them scared enough to desist (which then becomes part of their conspiracy theory): http://nymag.com/daily/intelligencer/2016/09/the-sandy-hook-hoax.html/.

[26] *Holocaust denial*, the denial of the systematic genocidal killing of millions of ethnic minorities in Europe by Nazi Germany in the 1930s and 1940s, is illegal in fourteen European nations. Many countries also have broader laws that criminalize genocide denial. Of the countries that ban Holocaust denial, some, such as Austria, Germany, Hungary, and Romania, were among the perpetrators of the Holocaust, and many of these also ban other elements associated with Nazism, such as the expression of Nazi symbols. Such laws do not exist in the U.S. or the U.K. https://en.wikipedia.org/wiki/Laws_against_Holocaust_denial.

[27] Asked about whether the rubber ducks had been poisoned, the sender of them said, "I think you could say they were 'weaponized,' when we rubbed them on our ball sacks." http://nymag.com/daily/intelligencer/2016/09/the-sandy-hook-hoax.html/

[28] I include a few in Recommended Readings, but there are many more good ones. See Berrett-Koehler's catalogue. Yes, they're my publisher, but it's because of the quality of their books that I'm proud to be one of their authors.

[29] See her wonderful book, *The Power to Transform: Leadership That Brings Learning and Schooling to Life* (San Francisco: Jossey-Bass, 2007). To learn more about her rich and varied career as a visionary educator, see http://www.stephaniepacemarshall.com/.

[30] Years ago when scenarios were popular, one of the founders of this process at Shell Oil Company, Napier Collins, told me that the only really useful scenarios were normative, those that focused people on what they wanted to create rather than simply reacting to the current environment. Seems useful to recall this power of intention and aspiration as we create islands of sanity.

[31] For more details, see http://www.sistersofsaintjosephfederation.org/about-us/history?id=372.

6. INTERCONNECTEDNESS

—

Nothing Living Lives Alone

When we try to pick out anything by itself, we find it hitched to everything else in the Universe.

— *John Muir,* conservationist

What Science Teaches

How do we understand life and the Universe? In twenty-first-century science, the very disparate fields of biology and physics have come to a shared understanding: everything we observe is not a separate "thing" but a participant in a vast web of relationships. Living systems and the Universe are best understood as dense layers of networked relationships. Even a single cell is a complex network, far beyond the imaginings of scientists until a few years ago. Nothing living lives alone. This shift in understanding became clear as the blinders of mechanistic thinking were torn off by the paradoxes revealed in scientific evidence.

Life insisted on being understood differently and everything changed. The pursuit of basic building blocks gave way to subatomic particles understood as bundles of energy potential that become visible only in relationship. (This is why there are particle colliders—no particle is visible until it collides with another energy at extreme high speeds.) Molecular biology, in its search to identify discrete genes as causal, as specific on and off switches, had to yield to the realization that genes are but one actor among DNA's many components—described by one scientist as an ensemble of actors.[1] Individual species, all plants and animals, lost their identity as individuals fighting against one another in the struggle for survival; now they are understood as necessary participants in an ecosystem where all benefit if balanced relationships are maintained. Even treasured theories of change changed, from linear incremental steps to observing that new systems suddenly arise through emergence.

What's interesting, as you'll read here, is how these two major sciences are coming to terms with the mysteries that life has presented them, and the meaning they infer from their observations.

Interconnectedness in Biology

As the system's view of life gained authority as the best explanatory lens for understanding how life works, it reframed the role of collaboration. Unlike our veneration of competition as the means to survive, collaboration is what is most essential to life's flourishing. Symbiosis is no longer a curious phenomenon but the fundamental process that spawns life, beginning at the microbial level, the process by which all complex ecosystems form.[2]

This fundamental shift introduced a type of ethics to biology. "Ethics is how we behave when we decide we belong together." With this ethic of collaboration, individual behavior takes on new meaning. As an organism interacts with its environment, individual actions impact the health of the ecosystem far beyond its nearest neighbors.[3]

Invasive species are destructive because they don't work from this ethic: They take everything for themselves and wreak havoc with their insatiable appetite. Predatory invaders destroy the delicate harmony and balance that an ecosystem has created for itself.

———

Collaboration is the process that creates an ecosystem; greed destroys it.

———

A system's view of life includes the qualities of harmony, balance, beauty—familiar experiences when we're gazing at mountains, flowers, streams, and everything else natural.[4] Darwin was astonished by beauty. In his journal in 1839 he wrote, "It is difficult to believe in the dreadful but quiet war of organic beings, going on in the quiet woods and smiling fields." He would have done well to relish the beauty and let go of the competition lens, but he could only perceive his experience through his worldview (although he seems to have toyed with this possibility in that smiling field).

When life was viewed as an assemblage of discrete parts, it was possible to study the parts in minute detail and never understand what we were studying. Its construction was understood. Numeric assessments of size, weight, and functions were easily obtained. Limited to quantification and separation, the information we gathered was appallingly inadequate for understanding life and how to work well with it. And without noticing systems of relationships, we were blind to qualities of harmony and beauty.

———

Conventional reductionist methods for understanding life turned it into a dull, uninteresting machine that we then felt free to abuse in any way that suited us.

———

Today, our world confronts us with an ironic conflict. We go into nature and feel a sense of harmony and profound belonging beyond the tiny confines of self. Yet our technology and the lives we live continue to demand that we perfect the means of extraction and destruction to keep our lives going. We ignore the science, destroy the environment, and then go outside to feel more peaceful.

The physicists are more puzzled by their experimental observations but, with them also, the revelation of mystery doesn't stop the production of more technologies that are facilitating ecological destruction.

Interconnectedness in Physics

What is often credited with being "the most astonishing discovery of twentieth-century physics"[5] is now, in the twenty-first century, the incessant evidence confronting physicists to rethink their fundamental assumptions about the Universe. The astonishing discovery was that the perceived separation of electrons does not mean they are separate. If two electrons have been paired, they continue to operate as one entangled whole even if the distance between them is the vastness of space. If the spin of one electron is changed, its pair changes instantly, faster than the speed of light. Bell's Theorem described this in 1964 and, since then, physical experiments continue to confirm that entanglement exists as an observable phenomenon. This raises the most profound questions about whether space exists.

Einstein was so disturbed by the possibility of entanglement that, just as Schrödinger had done for a different quantum observation, he created a thought experiment to show the absurdity of action-at-a-distance or nonlocality. He wanted to disprove the world that quantum theory pointed to: a reality that doesn't exist if it isn't being measured. Einstein wanted evidence of an objective reality. The EPR experiment[6] would prove that entities (particles) separated in space would still maintain their individual qualities, that there was a reality made up of independent things.

But the EPR thought experiment proved just the opposite.[7] There is no objective, independently existing reality that can be observed. If it can't be observed, there is no way of knowing whether it exists or not. But what could be observed was totally bizarre. Einstein labeled entanglement "spooky action at a distance," and he wasn't the only scientist spooked by the recurring evidence that the Universe does not operate as separate physical entities influencing each other through the laws of energy and motion, or influenced by force fields of gravity and electromagnetism. In classical physics, space matters: how far you are from the source determines the influence of these forces. Entanglement refutes spatial separation. Even when particles appear to be separated by space, they behave as one. Does this mean there is no space?

The EPR thought experiment set off many decades of research. Even though results were consistent and replicative (the mark of good science), scientists basically ignored nonlocality until the mid-1990s, when it became an accepted description of how the world operates at the quantum level. George Musser, a science writer and editor, notes, "I've spent time with scientists from a wide range of communities—people who study everything from subatomic particles to black holes to the grand structure of the cosmos. Over and over, I heard some variant of: 'Well, it's weird, and I wouldn't have believed it if I hadn't seen it for myself, but it looks like the world has just got to be nonlocal.'"[8]

The world thus appears as a complicated tissue of events, in which connections of different kinds alternate or overlap or combine and thereby determine the texture of the whole.

Werner Heisenberg, physicist

INTERCONNECTEDNESS

More than twenty different theories are being proposed to explain
entanglement, each of them more fanciful (and untestable) than the
next.[9] One scientist described the current state as "a chasm of mutual
incomprehension."[10] This is not surprising at a time when the very
foundations of physics are in question. When quantum mechanics first
displayed itself in experiments, Werner Heisenberg, one of the giants
in quantum physics, asked, "Can the universe possibly be so absurd as
it seemed to us in these atomic experiments?"[11] One thing is certain: a
reimagining of space is at the core of new physics.

In the midst of this profound upheaval, technology is keeping up with
quantum reality, and we are its beneficiaries. Theoretical physicists can't
explain what they're seeing, but applied physicists have been brilliant in
using what they don't understand to create new technologies. A brief list
of everyday things we now rely on that use quantum mechanics would
include transistors, computers, phones, electronics, lasers, MRIs, atomic
clocks. Seventy percent of our economy runs on quantum technologies.

Quantum physics didn't replace Newtonian physics. They both have
provided the means for this era of discovery and invention. But all
worldviews come to an end, just like everything else in life, and it appears
that we are at the end of the materialistic worldview of science which
was both magnificent and clunky. This view had built-in constraints of
matter, space, and time. They didn't appear as constraints when scientists
were drunk with discovery. Yet it is only Western science that has these
constraints—unwilling to acknowledge the presence of anything that
cannot be located in matter. This pursuit currently is very obvious in
neuroscientists who rejoice at the mapping of the brain in ever greater
detail but cannot describe how immaterial thoughts or consciousness
trigger reactions in the physical brain.

Western culture, now global, has paid a severe penalty for this materialistic obsession. Intuition, clairvoyance, precognition, mystical experiences, consciousness—these have each been discredited as "magic" and disparaged as the thinking of the poorly educated.[12] No self-respecting scientist would go near these.

And the reverse has also happened, with people seizing on quantum theory as the explanator of these phenomena, taking bits and pieces of the science to validate their experiences, labeling anything as "quantum" if it's the least bit puzzling or weird. Nobody has gained from these hijackings and misperceptions. Scientists continue to disparage the "New Agers" and they have a solid basis for their critiques, while those who want their work confirmed too often twist and misapply the science to suit their needs.

The world is not just a set of separately existing localized objects, externally related only by space and time. Something deeper, and more mysterious, knits together the fabric of the world.

Tim Maudlin, philosopher of physics

INTERCONNECTEDNESS

In recent years, this has improved. Some scientists have bravely explored the questions raised by entanglement even though, until recently, they often suffered rebuke and ostracism from others in their field. Dialogues between the Dalai Lama and preeminent scientists have explored the realms of consciousness, cognition, and the new physics.[13] Buddhist teachers trained as scientists have probed deeply into the corollaries and differences between the new physics and the 2,500-year-old science of mind that is Buddhism's unique contribution to human wisdom.[14]

This is a time of growing uncertainty. Physicists don't fuss with the mystery because they can make it work to produce new technologies.[15] These technologies, many of which breed destructive negative consequences while we grow more dependent on them, are the current Progress Trap. In contrast, scientists working with living systems theory *do* know what's going on: they have detailed and sufficient knowledge for how to keep ecosystems healthy. Their grief and anger only deepens as they see that science is not being applied with sufficient urgency or political will to prevent the destruction created by our insatiable predator species.

We have good reliable science on the workings of the biosphere, the ecospheres and our place within them. It is no surprise what is happening or who caused it—the Anthropocene Age is here. Science could have served us well. But it's not being allowed to contribute. How tragic. How stupid.

———

Now we have front row seats in the lessons of interconnectedness and the consequences of ignoring nature's fundamental truths. As the ecologists have noted: nature bats last.

When There Is No Place Called Home

Ours is a culture obsessed with the pursuit of happiness. As a consequence of this, we are more lonely, estranged, and lost than at any other time on this planet. The 32,000-year-old cave paintings and Paleolithic sites of paintings, pictographs, and petroglyphs all have handprints on the walls. Handprints, one on top of another, stamped there over tens of thousands of years, images from another time of togetherness.

How do we indicate we're together? Number of followers. Number of likes on a post. Being friended. A long Snapchat streak.[16] Nearly at the speed of light, we can tell our popularity. Some are entertained by these counts; others watch them obsessively and manipulate them so that, for a brief moment, they appear as the most popular. I got a glimpse of this well-developed craft when I was coached on how to promote a book using social media. I declined. Google and many businesses now offer tools for getting known and being most popular.

————

Popularity is not the same as feeling you belong. How sad if there's any confusion about this.

————

Two phrases I love that can never be used to describe cyberspace: "the dear neighbor" and "beloved community." How many remember what they mean? How many have never experienced such intimacy and connection, so the terms are poetic but meaningless?

In 2016, the furniture company IKEA did a survey among people aged 18–29 to learn what they felt about the concept of "home." Only 20 percent felt that home was an actual physical space; only 37 percent felt "at home" in their physical residences. The rest defined home as where they had their significant relationships. (Is that cafés, bars, gyms, concerts?) A full quarter of the survey's respondents said it was more important to have decent wi-fi "than to have social spaces in the home."[17] Not only do relationships zoom around the Web ungrounded, but younger people feel no need to create a physical place of their own where they can occur.

What happens when humans have no sense of place to call home? What happens when we no longer feel connected to others? The answers to these questions are found in the increasing suicide rates among youth, military veterans, farmers, indigenous peoples, and the elderly. Anywhere there is disconnection, there is suicide. As the isolation increases, so do suicide rates. These tragic statistics tell us that humans need to feel we belong. We need to be grounded in community.

We exist in a bundle of life. We say, "A person is a person through other people." It is not "I think therefore I am" [but rather] I am human because I belong. I participate, I share.

Archbishop Desmond Tutu

One time in Australia, when I was working in an Aboriginal community, I witnessed the strength that people gain when being on their ancestral ground. In town, in barren, bleak concrete buildings, people went about their work and nothing seemed amiss. But later in the day, having finished our meetings, we drove out to their original land, what they simply call "country." No pronouns, no adjectives—just "country." (When I Googled this to check my memory, I was taken to music sites.) My Aboriginal colleagues were transformed, filled with energy and humor. We had a great time, sitting together on the beach, hearing stories about fishing, feasts, and ocean storms.

It seemed clear that they were drawing energy from deep roots, tens of thousands of years that the land has held them in communion, no separation between Earth and human. This is how Aboriginal Australians describe their relationship to place, as an inseparable whole. As much as I have tried to understand what I witnessed, I know I never can. I was raised in a culture that makes a clear distinction between person and place. I was eager to leave home to be free to wander and work wherever I chose. Now I realize that such freedom comes at a price: I can never comprehend what it feels like to live as a settled community in trusted communion with the Earth.

When people with no ground or identity funnel their despair into violence and suicide, governments blame the victims and exert further police control. Predictably, social problems intensify; no one cares that these are legitimate responses to losing the strength of their ancestral lands.[18]

The same dynamic is playing out today in global culture, even if there's been no cultural tradition of place. Humans need to feel they belong. This is a real need that can never be satisfied virtually. Young people feel lost. What they find on the Internet—momentary friends, fans, pornography, empty entertainment, and extreme sensory stimulation—can never replace the sense of belonging that comes from living together in physical reality, participating together in all the dilemmas, dramas, and delights in the web of life.

A native community in the Northwest of Canada became well-known for putting an end to teen suicides after an epidemic of them. The solution became visible with this incident: A young man was standing on a bridge, about to throw himself into the river (ironically named the River of Life). While he stood there, perhaps hesitating, a car drove by and someone waved to him. That simple gesture stopped him. The community learned from his experience and thereafter focused efforts on how to create a culture of welcome and belonging. Teen suicides ceased.

One of our cultural identities or myths is of the one who goes it alone and pulls herself up by her bootstraps— the rebel, the outlaw, the self-made person. What a lie. What an ingratitude. What a danger. We are each the recipient of innumerable currents of life—through the lives of others—streaming into and influencing our own lives.

Geoffrey Shugen Arnold, Zen priest

Emergent Systems Can't Be Changed

Life doesn't change the way we want it to. Our costly attempts at organizational and social change have mostly failed because we made two mistakes. We tried to change individual behaviors, and we used linear approaches of goal setting, measurement and accountability. Logically, it all made good sense. Individual behaviors caused problems. Complex problems needed to be broken into chunks and then designated as tasks to specific individuals or teams. If everyone knew they would be held accountable for results, they'd be motivated to do the work. And change would happen.

This still seems like a reasonable strategy and is still the predominant approach, now assisted with project planning software and an *amazing* array of charts and graphics. Yet still our failures continue at an egregious rate. How many failed change strategies have you been involved in? When you think about it, it's probably a shocking number.

——

Life changes through emergence, not incrementally. Instead of the simple sum of individual parts, life mixes it all up in networks of relationships and produces something new.

——

Every part is playing its part, doing what it is created to do, communicating with its neighbors, adapting to environmental shifts. And then, quite suddenly, something else emerges that is unlike the parts that created it. Emergence always presents us with a surprise.

You may already understand this—many people have written about emergence, including me.[19] But I take delight in illustrating emergence with chocolate chip cookies. Consider the ingredients: flour, butter, eggs, water, salt, chocolate chips. None of them taste the way the cookie does; none of them can predict the flavor of the cookie. Yet when they all mix together in the right proportions, reliably and wondrously, you get a delicious cookie. It has a deliciousness that could never be predicted if you studied the parts, no matter the level of analysis. You can't find a cookie in the ingredients. And if you don't like the flavor—say, you put in too much salt—you can't remove that ingredient from the baked cookie. Once you've mixed the ingredients and baked them, you're stuck with the cookie. Hopefully you've got a great treat.

In the human sphere of organizing and living together, emergence isn't this delicious. Culture in any form, at any scale, is an emergent phenomenon. Once formed, you can't change it using reductionism. As Stephanie's story at the school illustrated, a culture of doubt, fear, and blame materialized from voicing emotional comments. No one person was responsible, and it would have been impossible to undo what had emerged by asking people to, post hoc, retract their comments. Stephanie had to notice the stories that had emerged. Once she saw them, she knew enough about emergence to use this time to invoke their core identity in order to change the story. The new story she proposed, The Gift, resonated with their identity and reenlivened the community to work together to resolve their current dilemma.

We spend so much time as individuals and leaders trying to undo things in order to fix them and create better alternatives. We were well schooled in reductionist thinking, have done it for years, so by now we're experts. We change the players, we focus on specific behaviors, we create new incentive systems for the same people. All for naught. The hard-to-accept news about emergence is that once a culture or pattern of response has emerged, you can't work backwards. There is nothing to do but start over.

We start over by returning to our identity, the source of self-organization, reclaiming what we still believe in, what description gives meaning to who we want to be. The nuns introduced me to the concept of "Refounding," a process described in Vatican II. Together they spent long hours contemplating the initial energy and inspiration of their founders, most of them teenage girls who ventured to the New World on faith alone. Drawing on those powerful ancestral currents, they could then discern how best to embody these in the present context. I have used this process many times with organizations and it always reestablishes direction and purpose in inspired, clear ways.

This is our work as leaders, to focus within our sphere of influence, accepting the harsh reality that we can't change the global culture that has emerged. There is no way to unwind where we are. We could have changed the "growth is good, extract everything you can" mindset when we were first warned of the impact this was having on the planet; Rachel Carson's *A Silent Spring* came out in 1962. We didn't. Some, like Exxon, learned in the 1980s of the potential environmental consequences from fossil fuels and switched from science to public relations and false science. Over many years, decisions made independently by governments and organizations, enabled by new technologies, emerged as global capitalism. And now we have this horrifying monster in our midst whose destructive powers are very evident but that cannot be tamed.

Emergence wields unusual power over the parts that created it. The term is *downward causation*. Even though the system wouldn't exist without the parts, once it does exist, it subjugates the parts. They now must participate in patterns of behavior foreign to them as individuals. In human cultures, this is easily visible. People adopt the morés of a culture, even those that contradict their personal values. Mostly these accommodations and changed behaviors go unobserved. The culture is in control, and most people unconsciously adapt. Some see how they're changing but pay the price of compliance in order to belong, even if they don't like what they belong to.

Yet everything alive possesses the freedom to choose what to notice and determine its response. At any moment, we can use our intelligence to notice that we can't abide how this culture is changing us, our children, and colleagues.

———

Freeing ourselves from an emergent culture is an act of conscious rebellion. We know we cannot change what's emerged, so we walk out of it to begin again. What will emerge as we reclaim life-affirming identities? What new culture will form in ourselves, our families, our organizations? It all depends on the values we embed at the start.

———

If we embed ecological values, if we focus on relationships, if we position learning as a core value, if we seek to behave as partners with life, then we have a strong chance to manifest, to self-organize as individuals living and working purposefully together in healthy community.

How wonderful to be able to see clearly, choose consciously, and know what to do.

Leading with Emergence

So many words are tossed around these days describing life and organizational change. "It's a dynamic situation." "It's very organic." "Things are self-organizing." "We're using an emergent design."

I suppose it's possible to take the use of these terms—all from the science of living systems—as an indication we're changing our paradigm. But more frequently I see them as a veneer on old behaviors—we just sound cool using them.

What does it mean to say, "The situation is dynamic"? I think it means we have no idea what's going to happen next and that's just the way it is.

How often do you hear (or say), "It is what it is"? Does this indicate that we're feeling peaceful or hopelessly resigned to our fate? I've been with people (mostly Buddhist teachers) who say, "As it is" and radiate peace; I feel they are present and available as they say this. But usually people who use this phrase say it with a shoulder shrug or gesture of helplessness. It's become such a common phrase (and so annoying?) that the comedian Stephen Colbert joked, "Those who say, 'It is what it is' will be hit with 'it' but not told 'what' it was."

———

The dynamics of living systems provide the means to foster good work and healthy relationships. But we have to understand them beyond casually applied adjectives.

What does it mean to work with emergence, life's true source of dynamic, organic, self-organizing change? I used to joke that calling something "an emergent process" was just a scientific term for "making it up as we go along," or "flying by the seat of our pants." (That's a very strange phrase, isn't it?) Working with emergence means we are fully engaged, carefully observing what's going on as we do our work, learning from experience, applying those learnings, adapting, changing. In other words, behaving like everything else alive does.

Life *is* dynamic, changing frequently and surprisingly. But it's not really a mystery. Life is lawful—there is a reliable logic to the laws of nature, cause and effect. Life's surprises aren't surprising—we just weren't paying attention to the right things. We get blindsided, but life does not act blindly or randomly. It is possible to understand the multiple causes that were the source of our surprise. We simply need to engage our intelligence, open our perceptions, get past our close mindedness, and ask, What just happened? Why do we think it happened?

Systems emerge through the complexity of interactions among the participants, each of whom is choosing what to notice and how to respond. Those individual responses link together into patterns of behaviors that, at the human level, are best described as culture. Once the system emerges, downward causation is in effect, and the culture is the primary influence over individuals. Now it's too late to change.

———

The critical action for leaders is to ensure that what gets set in motion at the start of an organizing effort is healthy. The "self" of self-organization is the critical variable.

What are the values, intentions, principles for behavior that describe who we want to be? Once established, are these common knowledge, known by all? As we work together, do we refer to our identity to make decisions? How do we respond when something goes wrong? Do we each feel accountable for maintaining the integrity of this identity?

You may notice that the questions I ask you to consider throughout this book have a similar focus. This is intentional. These questions lie at the epicenter of creating a healthy self-organizing group or organization. They bring us back to alert, open behaviors—the true sanity of any living system. A living system is a learning system.

If we are working well with emergence, these questions become part of our everyday perceptions. We don't ask them occasionally or once a year at a retreat. We all have to become more observant, more open to differing perceptions, more open to new interpretations. However, only the leader is in the position to see the whole of the organization. No matter how willing people might be, everyone is overwhelmed and consumed with their own work. Sane leadership is developing the capacity to observe what's going on in the whole system and then either reflect that back or bring people together to consider where we are now.

This is working with emergence. And self-organization. In a dynamic, organic way.

The Causes of Suffering

Many years ago,
the Dalai Lama asked a group of professionals
(including friends who told me this story)
"What is the cause of suffering?"
Everybody had an answer:
Poverty. Injustice. War. Alienation. Racism.
After listening to their answers,
he abruptly interrupted them.
No, he said,
the cause of suffering
is when good people
begin their work together
and then fail to notice
what is arising between them.

The Joy of Interbeing[20]

In the pursuit of happiness, we estrange ourselves from joy.

Once you've known joy, you are no longer confused about the difference. Joy is a sensation of your entire being, difficult to describe in words but similarly known by anyone who's experienced it. The experience of joy often feels the same as sadness.

In my own experience, joy and sadness are the same—my being feels embraced and alive. I am present with energy beyond what my physical body can contain yet it does. I am laughing. I am crying. It doesn't matter which.

———

I know joy to be the experience of connection, communion, presence, grace, as it is.

———

My own experiences have helped me understand what others describe as their most joyful moments: the birth of a baby, your own or a child's wedding, working in a natural disaster or a situation of great human suffering.

How can joy be available in moments of great suffering? All around you lives are threatened, unstoppable destructive forces are at work, everyone is stretched beyond physical limits to help, rescue, save. For the rest of their lives, people will recall the intensity and horror. And the joy.

The presence of joy even in the worst experiences is explained in this biblical promise: "Whenever two or more are gathered, there will I be also." Joy arises from self-transcendence. We transcend the limits of self. We transcend our needs for personal safety or caution. We discover new powers, new ways of being.

Joy is a reliable consequence of self-transcendence. In the worst conditions, our most noble human qualities are right there, offering us the capacity to help, to strengthen, to love, to console. Joy is an experience of what scientists are struggling to understand: the dance of energies never separated celebrating this as true.

———

Beyond this tiny, puny self we've been protecting, we enter sacred world, the bundle of belonging, returned to one another by being fully present for one another.

———

The mystical traditions of all spiritual faiths describe the experience— again beyond words—of oneness or, as a Buddhist teacher said, of zeroness. In the mystical state, there is a self, but not. There is experience that "I" am having, but it's not "I." There is vastness, luminosity, evenness, bliss, peace—but it's impossible to locate who is experiencing it.

I slept and dreamt that life was joy.
I awoke and saw that life was service.
I acted and behold, service was joy.

Rabindranath Tagore

INTERCONNECTEDNESS: RESTORING SANITY

The Universe has revealed itself in mystical experiences to human ancestors long before we sapiens took over. Now we seem locked into our version of *sapien*-ness, exploring the sacred world with our analytic science. I don't see how scientists can ever understand their experimental findings and models until they honor the fact that humans have been exploring the same questions for hundreds of thousands of years and arrived at different ways of knowing. Their answers cannot be dismissed as magic. In truth, our present culture is the one engaged in magical thinking, believing we're going to find a way out of this mess with technology and science.

I am not interested in romanticizing indigenous wisdom. Like all humans, their civilizations took the same reliable path to collapse. What I am interested in is to enlarge our understanding of how this world works. We're only the latest manifestation of humans asking that question and our arrogance is astonishing.

———

Linda Hogan, of the Chickasaw people, describes our Western ways as "primitive." We don't understand how the world works, this web of life rich in species beyond number, each using their intelligence to find their place as neighbors.

We Live by Different Stories

What finally turned me back toward the older traditions
of my own [Chickasaw] and other Native peoples was the
inhumanity of the Western world, the places—both inside
and out—where the culture's knowledge and language
don't go, and the despair, even desperation, it has spawned.
We live, I see now, by different stories, the Western mind
and the indigenous. In the older, more mature cultures
where people still live within the kinship circles of animals
and human beings there is a connection with animals,
not only as food, but as 'powers,' a word which can be
taken to mean states of being, gifts, or capabilities.

Linda Hogan, "First People"[21]

You Can't Build on Broken

When a biologist encounters an ecosystem in trouble, she/he will pay close attention to what has broken in the pattern of relationships among diverse species. Health will be restored by creating new connections and strengthening existing ones. This solution is found in the etymology of the word health. It comes from an old English word for wholeness. That word comes from an earlier word for holiness. Whenever two or more are gathered. . . .

For many years, the Berkana Institute (I'm co-founder and serve again as president) proclaimed, "Whatever the problem, community is the answer." I learned this working in southern Africa, among indigenous communities in many places and, time after time, from my now dear friend, Angela Blanchard. We met in New Orleans sixteen months after Katrina. Angela's organization had been intimately involved in immediately settling the more than 120,000 people who had to flee New Orleans after the storm and find refuge in Houston.

Angela has led Neighborhood Centers Inc. (NCI) in Houston for more than thirty years. Houston is the second-fastest-growing city in America and one of the most diverse. It has the same issues as other urban centers— exciting growth coupled with increasing economic disparity, poverty in the midst of plenty. What began as a settlement house in 1907 has grown into one of the largest nonprofits in the United States, serving "new neighbors" of immigrants coming into Houston, as well as those long-marginalized. The range of services covers all ages and most needs, from health and education to job training and placement. I love how they describe their work because they actually do this: "We believe that our neighborhoods are bridges to opportunity, that people can transform communities and that everyone everywhere has something to contribute. For Good."

They serve in more than seventy community locations. There are six main centers, two built as village squares that house a broad range of services in brightly painted, human-scale buildings. Angela has stewarded this extraordinary growth and contribution by relying on community. She summarizes her experience in a simple phrase: Every person has the desire to "Earn, Learn, and Belong." (In 2016, she brought this learning to refugee settlements in Europe, working with on-the-ground leaders to create places first of welcome and then long-term communities.) I encourage you to read about the work of NCI on their beautiful website, filled with the faces and stories of the more than 500,000 people they serve so well.[22] You will learn and see how healthy vibrant communities are being built among diverse people, relying on the aspirations we all share as human human beings.

———

"You can't build on broken" is one of Angela's best slogans. It's the recipe for building healthy community.

———

Like the biologists, but unlike the common approaches in aid and development efforts worldwide, health is found in working with the strengths already present and creating new connections. If you're building a new community center, ask people to design it by bringing in photos of what they love about their community. If you're developing job training programs, get jobs guaranteed from corporate partners before training starts. If you want immigrants to become legal, bring in federal immigration authorities to advise them directly. Tragically, this cooperation is no longer possible with new anti-immigration policies.

When you strengthen connections, even among those who have been indifferent or hostile, you create possibilities. We may be strangers or estranged, but we can become neighbors if we decide to work together on building something good. For good.

We may have known this truth but now forgotten it in our devastatingly polarized society. Too often our energies have been diverted into strategies of protection from the opposition and winning the endless battles. We couldn't avoid this, but now it's time to remember the value of community. In so many situations, I've witnessed Angela's unshakable faith in people materialize as gifts and contributions that create community. I've learned again that community is the answer.

Angela always speaks of grace and joy—gifts abundant when we are working together. As we gather together to create islands of sanity, we, too, will have many moments of grace and joy. Guaranteed.

———

We are not broken people. It's our relationships that need repair. It's relationships that bring us back to health, wholeness, holiness.

———

Intelligence

we are told how wrong it is to impute
our intelligence to animals
building them up raising their ranking
attributing behaviors meant only for us

but what if we were as intelligent as animals?

if we had their intelligence
we would not push away
what we don't want to know
we'd know denial is a form of suicide

if we had their intelligence
we would notice who's around us
no longer duped into thinking
we can make it on our own

if we had their intelligence
we would engage with everything
mindfulness not a fad knowing
staying awake means staying alive

we are a young species
we would be wiser if we
recognized our immaturity
and used our intelligence
to take our right place on the planet

Margaret Wheatley, How Does Raven Know?

INTERCONNECTEDNESS: NOTES

[1] The Genome Project led to the discovery of epigenetics, that DNA can be changed by the behaviors and experiences of individuals. The ensemble metaphor is from Richard Frances, *Epigenetics: The Ultimate Mystery of Inheritance* (New York: Norton, 2011).

[2] See *Symbiotic Planet*, Lynn Margulis. Her revolutionary theory about the microcosmos of bacteria was at first ridiculed and now is foundational among biologists; a new Tree of Life published in 2016 has bacteria in most of life's branches. Carl Zimmer, "Scientists Unveil New 'Tree of Life,'" nytimes.com, April 17, 2016.

[3] A remarkable video, "How Wolves Change Rivers," provides a dramatic example of what are termed "trophic cascades."

[4] The Greeks believed in sacred geometry, that harmony and beauty are properties of the world independent of our observations, but that we all respond to. God was the grand geometer, creating geometric forms that give the experience of harmony. Sacred geometry is found in the patterns used in many cultures for sacred buildings, paintings, and symbolic art.

[5] Tim Maudlin, a leading philosopher of physics, in George Musser, *Spooky Action at a Distance* (New York: Scientific American/Farrar, Straus & Giroux, 2015), p. 11.

[6] Proposed in 1935, by Albert Einstein, Boris Podolsky, and Nathan Rosen.

[7] This happens often in theoretical physics: an experiment set up to prove the impossibility of a quantum phenomenon instead establishes further proof of its existence. It happened to Schrodinger, Einstein, and Wheeler, among the most prominent quantum theorists, and also to others intent on proving that the world wasn't as weird as it appeared to be. It was and it is. See Musser, *Spooky Action at a Distance.*

[8] Musser, *Spooky Action at a Distance*, p. 10. As you'll note from the number of quotes, I find Musser's book invaluable and up-to-date (2015). He offered a brilliant presentation on nonlocality at Google in February 2016, "Spooky Action at a Distance." https://www.youtube.com/watch?v=D8nqgyBsM9U.

[9] Roger Penrose, one of the leading physicists, published *Fashion, Faith, and Fantasy in the New Physics of the Universe* in 2016. The title speaks for itself.

[10] Musser, *Spooky Action at a Distance*, p. 115.

[11] *Leadership and the New Science* (3rd ed.), p. 6.

[12] See Dean Radin, *Entangled Minds: Extrasensory Experiences in a Quantum Reality* (New York: Paraview Pocket Books, 2006).

[13] See the Mind and Life Institute, founded in 1990. Dialogues occur annually; these began in the mid-1980s by Adam Engle and Francisco Varela working in close partnership with the Dalai Lama.

[14] See Recommended Readings.

[15] James Kakalios in *Scientific American*, 2010, http://www.scientificamerican.com/article/everyday-quantum-physics/.

[16] A Snapchat streak, indicated by a fire emoji, is when you have exchanged snaps three days in a row. The goal is to keep the streak alive for as long as possible. At the end of 2016, Snapchat rebranded itself as Snap, now selling spectacles from vending booths that, at the press of a button on the glasses, will videotape where you are and immediately download the video onto your phone to send to all your friends. One commentator noted that young people now communicate through pictures rather than words. OMG.

[17] See http://www.curbed.com/2016/6/20/11978178/ikea-life-at-home-report-2016.

[18] See, for example: "The Town Where 100 Young People Have Tried to Kill Themselves," www.bbc.com, August 21, 2016.

[19] My book *So Far from Home* details that the things we activists have been focused on changing are emergent phenomena. What emerges can't be changed by working backward to change the parts.

[20] The great Vietnamese Buddhist teacher Thich Nhat Hahn founded the Order of Interbeing. The word itself means many things but conveys immediately our interconnectedness. It also can be used as a verb: "We interare."

[21] In *Intimate Nature: The Bond Between Women and Animals* (New York: Fawcett Books, 1999). I have found deep comfort in Hogan's book, *Dwellings: A Spiritual History of the Living World* (New York: Norton, 2007).

[22] This is a state-of-the-art website, visually delightful and as welcoming as the centers themselves: www.neighborhood-centers.org.

7. WHO DO WE CHOOSE TO BE?

Each time we collide with the real, we deepen our understanding of the world and become more fully a part of it.

— Nicholas Carr

Leadership and the Collapse of Complexity

We are not the first leaders to be stewarding a time of disintegration, fear, and loss. But none of us has been prepared for where we are. If we are older, we honed our leadership skills in a time of growth and possibility, when change was in the air and everything seemed possible. New paradigms led to new processes; new processes of systems thinking and participation yielded great results. Growth seemed good, and even as we were increasingly aware of the suffering of those far from us, our lives kept moving forward in a good way. Many of us heard and responded to the cries of the world. We took on the work of addressing urgent problems of the environment, turbo capitalism, human rights, poverty, health, the marginalized and oppressed.

This is what I remember vividly about the world I lived and worked in before 9/11. I was hopeful we would change the world—an attitude I have long since rejected as a distraction and waste of energy. We were confident that change was possible. It was possible because we were talented, dedicated, and caring people, armed with new tools of systems thinking, wise about human motivation, trained in the skills of participation, listening, conversation, community building. As leaders, we were smart enough to figure things out, to organize and mobilize on behalf of worthy causes. We would create positive change. Without a doubt.

Do you remember this era of confidence and how it impacted you as a leader, citizen, parent, activist? (It's easy for me: I only have to reread my earlier writings that exuded such confidence. I know I'm not romanticizing how I felt in that era.)

Then 9/11 happened and showed us where we were in the pattern of collapse. In Glubb's stages, we are in the Age of Decadence, too self-absorbed or distractedly entertained to notice the impacts we are having on the greater world beyond ourselves. Feasting on empty superficial nutrients, we failed to notice what our lifestyles were costing others (and ourselves). The planet and many of its peoples were suffering from our insatiable habits. I don't mean to simplify the complexity of issues that led to the 9/11 attacks, but one thing became crystal-clear: we are a civilization in collapse and the barbarians have moved in on us.

Human societies always arrive at this place. It begins when we grow too large to remain as a community of intimate relationships. We shift from the bonds of community to hierarchy; we organize into complex social relationships, with many different institutional structures and roles. Complexity increases as more roles and structures are created—this sociopolitical structure is the definition of complexity used to describe civilizations. Increasing differentiation leads to the need for controls; policies and regulations are necessary to make the many varied parts work together.

———

At some point, the complexity overwhelms the civilization. It can no longer afford to maintain the society it created. It can no longer feed the beast.

At this point, leaders desperate to maintain control do three stupid things, each intended to preserve their power. First, they engage in wars, which may rally patriotism but drain the budget and destroy lives. (The wars are paid through increased taxation of the lower classes and printing money.) Second, they buy off the populace with meaningless entertainments, entitlements, and promises that can never be kept. Third, they create a false sense of reality by inflating the economy. The true costs of resources are masked by printing money, offering loose credit, and taking a deliberate economic approach that creates a false sense of prosperity.

Those who direct the affairs of a mature civilization are engaged in a war against reality that they cannot win, because a series of insidious transformations has rendered the society dysfunctional and ungovernable.

William Ophuls

As good leaders, not stupid ones, we may be fully aware of what's going on, how economic and social policies are failing to solve our problems, increasing people's anger and alienation; we may even be fearing social revolt.[1] But again, I want to remind you that what you just read is true of all civilizations, not just ours. We are not the first to be here. We cannot fix this disaster by our own leadership, no matter how good and sane we are.

A society has collapsed when it displays a rapid, significant loss of an established level of sociopolitical complexity. Collapse is the sudden simplification of complexity, the loss of institutions and ways of life that depend on complex systems to do their work, deliver services, transport goods. (Y2K was based on the scenario of total systems collapse when global computer systems were projected to stop functioning at midnight 2000 from programs that could not deal with a four-digit year, but collapse was avoided by intensive remediation of computer systems.) While collapse affects all spheres of human endeavor, it is primarily a fundamental failure in the social and political spheres. The loss of capacity is quite rapid as the failures of interlocking systems create a cascade effect.

The loss of complex systems pushes people back on their own resources; they retreat into clans and ethnicities. Historically, people revert to the worst human behaviors, struggling to survive such great dislocation. A few people step forward to do what they can, acting heroically and embodying the qualities of compassion and insight.

———

Now, who do you choose to be as a leader for this time?

The Shambhala Warriors

There comes a time when all life on Earth is in danger.

Great barbarian powers have arisen.

Although these powers spend their wealth

in preparations to annihilate one another,

they have much in common:

Weapons of unfathomable destructive power,

and technologies that lay waste our world.

In this era when the future of sentient life hangs by the

frailest of threads, the kingdom of Shambhala emerges.[2]

The kingdom of Shambhala describes an enlightened people, whether as fact or myth, in far distant history. At the time described in this prophecy, the warriors come forth. According to Tibetan teachers, that time is now.

The warriors are well positioned; they are working within the halls of power, so they know how these systems work. They see clearly how the practices and ambitions of these systems are deadening the human spirit and threatening all of life. They recognize that these destructive practices are the result of wrong thinking. Therefore, they can be dismantled by the human mind as well.

———

The Warriors are armed with only two weapons: compassion and insight. They are peaceful warriors, vowing to never use aggression or fear to accomplish their ends.

———

As Sir John Glubb noted, without naming them this, spiritual warriors always arise during collapse: "While despair might permeate the greater part of the nation, others achieved a new realization of the fact that only readiness for self-sacrifice could enable a community to survive. Some of the greatest saints in history lived in times of national decadence, raising the banner of duty and service against the flood of depravity and despair."

Naming Ourselves

Many years ago, I listened as Reverend Wayne Muller challenged people to choose a name for themselves big enough to contain their entire life. He said that so many of the names we select speak to challenges we've overcome—cancer, war, abuse, addiction—but that these hard-won names aren't big enough for the remainder of our lives. Over the years, I've added to his challenge by asking everyone to choose a name that draws us forward into the future, a name that requires us to be fearless.

I took this challenge personally and, as I began understanding where we are in the pattern of collapse, I began searching for a name to prepare me for the future I saw coming. None of my previous incarnations were sufficient. In fact, they were quite limiting. I had been a consultant, educator, advisor—good roles designed to fix things. I had been a writer and speaker—good roles for inspiring others to fix things.

When I gave up saving the world, I turned away from these professional tags and began to seek role models in those who had lived through terrible collapse. For grievous loss of life and the deliberate destruction of a culture and spiritual tradition, I looked to the Dalai Lama of Tibet. For the dedication, intelligence, and perseverance of a century-long struggle, I looked to Nelson Mandela and Archbishop Tutu of South Africa. These are not minor role models, and I don't mean to sound pretentious. I had the privilege to learn firsthand from the monks who fled Chinese destruction by walking for months over the snowy Himalayas to preserve their precious teachings. I learned from many South African colleagues of the price they paid—imprisonment, torture, exile—to claim their freedom. I am more intimate with the nature of their struggles than others and still keep close watch on what's happening in both countries.

There were thousands of others I could have looked to for guidance, and I read many stories of heroism from the two world wars, the civil rights movement, the farmworkers' movement, and current global work with refugees and women and children. I feel drawn to these stories because we need to learn from them. We need to learn that it is possible to persevere in very difficult conditions, and that the struggles reward us with deep relationships that offer us moments of joy and gladness even in hellish situations.

———

Who are the warriors in your own family? Soldiers, immigrants, those who experienced injustice and refused to yield, those who had strong values and embodied them. . . . Who are they?

———

I am not preparing myself or you for martyrdom, but I am intent on creating a different reference point for our work going forward. We are part of a noble tradition of people who, in every age, devote themselves to protecting and serving others. The costs of that service vary widely, as will ours. I just want us to be part of those who "raise the banner of duty and service against the flood of depravity and despair."

And what is our cause? It is the unshakable belief that human beings are worth our last ounce of energy. We make the choice to be there to preserve, protect, defend, champion, encourage, honor the human spirit.

The name I have chosen for myself that calls me to be fearless is a *Warrior for the Human Spirit*. Perhaps it sounds a bit dramatic, but it has a simple definition:

A Warrior for the Human Spirit is a decent human being who aspires to be of service in an indecent, inhumane time.

Warriors remember what it means to behave decently, ethically. We remember the capacities that every human being possesses. We affirm and work with these forgotten qualities through our presence and our wise actions. And in all we do, we consciously try to refrain from adding to the confusion, aggression, and fear overwhelming most people.

The warrior tradition is found in many cultures, focused either on defense or peaceful service. In Tibetan, the word for warrior, *pawo*, means one who is brave, brave enough to never resort to aggression or fear to accomplish their purposes. In all traditions, warriors are a highly specialized group of people who are devoted to selfless service, who train with discipline and diligence to develop their skills, and who band together as a community. Warriors for the Human Spirit train in service to people, to support our best human capacities for generosity, compassion, altruism, curiosity, creativity, caring.

Movies are filled with images of warriors as relentless agents of violence defending helpless people. In real life, even when engaged in violence, warriors are not undisciplined actors of aggression. In the greatest warrior traditions, such as the Samurai and Special Forces in the military, warriors train with great devotion and discipline. Whatever their weapons—violence or peace—they are well prepared and in control of themselves. This is why they train constantly.

—

Throughout time, warriors arise when the people need protection.

—

There is a strong code of ethics that binds them together in honor to their cause and to one another. Honor codes and strong ethics characterize those in the Age of Conquest intent on using violent means to destroy the decadent culture. A sense of honor and strong ethics appear again among those few people who, at the end of the cycle, seek to alleviate the suffering caused by collapse, not with violence but with compassion and insight.

The Dalai Lama's Principles for Ethical Strategies[3]

- Ensure that compassion is the motivation.

- Any problem must take into account the big picture and long-term consequences rather than short-term feasibility.

- In applying reason, we must stay honest, unbiased, and self-aware, vigilant to avoid self-delusion.

- Stay humble—know the limits of our knowledge and also realize we can easily be misguided in a rapidly changing reality.

- The foremost concern is the well-being of humanity and the planet we inhabit.

The Great Binding Law
The Constitution of the Iroquois Nation Confederation[4]

The thickness of your skin shall be seven spans—which is to say that you shall be proof against anger, offensive actions, and criticism. Your heart shall be filled with peace and good will and your mind filled with a yearning for the welfare of the people of the Confederacy. With endless patience you shall carry out your duty and your firmness shall be tempered with tenderness for your people. Neither anger nor fury shall find lodgments in your mind and all your words and actions shall be marked with calm deliberation. In all of your deliberations in the Confederate Council, in your efforts at law making, in all your official acts, self-interest shall be cast into oblivion.

Cast not over your shoulder behind you the warnings of the nephews and nieces should they chide you for any error or wrong you may do, but return to the way of the Great Law which is just and right. Look and listen for the welfare of the whole people and have always in view not only the present but also the coming generations, even those whose faces are yet beneath the surface of the ground—the unborn of the future Nation.

What Do You Stand For?

Let me begin, in the spirit of the TV show *Mission Impossible*, "Should you choose to accept this mission, . . ."

To take on the name and role of <u>Warrior for the Human Spirit</u> is not an impossible mission. It's just our turn. But it represents a serious departure from prior roles and identities. This new role requires unshakable faith and confidence in the human spirit. It would be good to contemplate why you're considering it.

———

What in your past experiences has led you to want to be someone who protects and champions people? What have you personally observed and learned about people and our capabilities? Are people really worth struggling for?

———

The Bible describes faith as "the evidence of things unseen which are true." As we read the headlines, watch the news, sit in meetings that turn ugly, witness aggressive behavior everywhere (including kids' movies), our faith in human goodness can be challenged every day. Goodness can go unnoticed in this current environment, which is why we need faith that goes beyond appearances. But our faith is not unfounded. Daily we receive gifts of generosity that, if noticed, tune us into the deeper reality of who we humans also are. We can be provoked to aggression and hatred, and we can be moved to self-sacrifice and caring.

"Random acts of kindness" really aren't so random—they're reliable glimpses into our better human natures. Yet even with deep faith, it requires enormous courage to take a stand these days. It is impossible not to have a target placed on you when you champion a cause. In the pre-Internet days, leaders who stood up for people and new ways of operating were ignored, made fun of, or told to cease their efforts. If none of these attempts silenced them, the tactics switched to slander—the personhood of the leader became the target of attack. Now, everyone who takes a stand for something good receives far worse than slander: they can expect death threats and hate hurled at them through the Internet, and whole social media campaigns mobilized against them. If you're lucky, you don't become part of a conspiracy theory that twists your intentions into something diabolic.

In this current environment, it is faith that provides the deeper ground for our actions. We can expect to be misunderstood and victimized for our good efforts. If we're lucky, we just get ignored, left to ourselves, below the radar. This is a real blessing—although it requires giving up any needs for approval and recognition. But if we do get on the radar, in this climate of careless fear mongering and hate, we have to be prepared for unjust and possibly insane reactions to our work.

Warriors for the Human Spirit are awake human beings who have chosen not to flee. They abide.

A South African Warrior-in-Training

Where Do You Stand?

Recall the words of President Teddy Roosevelt at the beginning of this book: "Do what you can, with what you have, where you are." If we sign on as Warriors for the Human Spirit, we don't have to go looking for opportunities to defend and protect people. Opportunities are everywhere, created by decisions and policies that blithely ignore people and their concerns or want them out of the picture. People have disappeared from the decision-making equation—it's as if there are robots doing the work.

And now, more companies envision just such a blissful future of robots and artificial intelligence that eliminates people completely. The global company Uber, which began as a human-centered company offering income opportunities to people as taxi drivers, is converting to electric cars. Their dream is to take over urban transport with driverless vehicles. "Uber's cars . . . will actively be competing with and making irrelevant the moms and students and two-job-hustlers Uber has long held up as the human capital that make its platform so compelling."[5]

Beyond the dreams of automating humans away, there are still the work environments in both the Global South and North that make their profits on degrading people to the level of machines: endlessly repetitive rote labor in terrible conditions for inhumane lengths of time. Even where people earn good wages, such as tech startups, the demands on people and their treatment is a shocking indication that bright young entrepreneurs view people as an inconvenient necessity, at least for now.[6]

Wherever you're working is where you take a stand. You don't have to go looking for new places, other issues, compelling causes. If you're in a school, a financial firm, the UN, a refugee camp, a small nonprofit, a church, a hospital—wherever you are, stay there and notice the abundance of warrior opportunities. It may well be that you're already operating in this way—speaking up against unjust actions, influencing policies to address root causes, reminding decision makers what statistics mean in terms of human costs, going to bat for a colleague who's been wrongfully harmed by administrative action, calling attention to new populations that need services, bearing witness to those whose suffering cannot be solved, comforting a sorrowful person or child.

———

What's common in all these actions is that human beings are at the center. By our actions, we call attention to people and their suffering. And we act where we can to support and console those near us.

———

Although you've been doing these things, what's different is the role we have chosen for ourselves. Instead of being a team player or a person who may quietly, casually raise these issues, we make these actions primary. If we don't speak up, who will? Where are the others who are championing the human spirit?

But we must choose our actions wisely.

The two skills of the warrior are compassion and insight. Compassion is easy—it arises spontaneously from an open heart. Insight or discernment requires more skill. We have to choose our battles. Or wording that in less aggressive terms, we have to discern where we can be most effective. Good thinking is required. Understanding the opposition is required. Finding one's allies is essential. Right timing is everything.

We're not sitting on a high horse in full armor ready to charge. We're trying to be the presence of sanity. And for this, we need to develop new skills.

—

To be present for others, or for a situation, we have to clear our perceptual filters. We have to discern as clearly as possible what is going on. Today, we are fortunate to have many means to develop more direct perception, free of me. This is not some new technology. It's found in the richness of offerings under the category of mindfulness practices. These practices teach us to watch our minds, notice what triggers us, and learn how to create a space before reacting. In addition to mindfulness practices, there are more specific practices for dealing with difficult emotions and personal triggers. So much is out there—the only challenge is for you to find one or more that you can work with and create a disciplined practice.

These are the practices that give us the ability to stay present, even when challenged by other people's aggression and fear. These abilities require disciplined training. You can't just will yourself to be present—you need to know yourself well enough to notice you've just been triggered.

As you become familiar with your habitual patterns of behavior and what triggers you, it becomes possible to shift from reaction to response. You will still be triggered, but you learn to know these as warning signs to yourself. It's time to sit back (mentally or physically) and let your mind move past this moment of high emotion. If you pause, your mind slows down and becomes more spacious. Within that space you can find responses that create possibility rather than aggression.

The intent of any mindfulness practice is to learn to know yourself, not to become peaceful. Knowing how your own mind works makes it possible to stay present and engaged in hypercharged situations without losing your cool.

———

Over time, as we get to know our minds well, we learn to trust ourselves. We know our usual reactions and have brought them under control. I've found that I can now go willingly into situations that, in the past, were guaranteed to trigger a flood of difficult emotions: anger, grief, rage, despair. I had a great desire to be in those places, but until I trained my mind, I couldn't trust myself. Angered at an injustice, I would aggressively launch a counterattack. Yet I had pledged not to add any more aggression to the world. Encountering a scene of great suffering, I would be overcome by fear and despair. Yet I had vowed not to add to the fear in the world or to let it disable me.

Developing a stable mind is the core work of training oneself to be a warrior.

There is no other way to prepare oneself for the difficulties, tragedies, and insanity that will continue to escalate. We can't change this world, but we can change ourselves so that we can be of service to this world.

You have to take a stand, and stand there.

Daniel Ellsberg, activist priest

The Faith and Confidence of Warriors

- We have unshakable confidence that people can be kinder, gentler, and wiser than our current society tells us we are. We rely on human goodness and offer this faith as a gift to others.

- We offer ourselves not as activists to change the world, but as compassionate presences and trustworthy companions to those suffering in this world. We embody compassion without ambition.

- Our confidence, dignity, and wakefulness radiate out to others as a beacon of who we humans are.

- Our confidence is not conditioned by success or failure, by praise or blame. It arises naturally as we see clearly into the nature of things.

- We create an atmosphere of compassion, confidence, and upliftedness with our very presence.

- We create a good human society wherever we are, whenever we can, with the people and resources that are available to us now.

- We rely on joy arising, knowing it is never dependent on external circumstances but comes from working together as good human beings.

- We encounter life's challenges with a sense of humor, knowing that lightness and play increase our capacity to deal with suffering.

The Gift of Meaningful Work

In a world preoccupied with meaningless tasks, people are ever more eager to engage in work that offers a chance to contribute, to remember how good it is to be a thinking, contributing colleague. These days, having one good conversation can reintroduce us to what it feels like to be in a satisfying human relationship. The same is true when we have the opportunity to think together and come up with a solution to a troubling situation. The human qualities that have become distant memories, or never known at all, come flooding in when we work together for a common purpose. Meaningful work reawakens us to what it feels like to be human human beings.

Throughout the years leading up to Now, the dream has been to free people from work and give them more leisure. This made sense, and still does, for those toiling in hot fields, in mines deep within the earth, on factory assembly lines, or any job that is dull, repetitive, exhausting, demeaning. In 1930, John Maynard Keynes dreamed a dream of the future: "For the first time since his creation man will be faced with his real, his permanent problem, how to use his freedom from pressing economic cares, how to occupy the leisure, which science and compound interest will have won for him, to live wisely and agreeably and well."[7]

In 1957, a *New York Times Book Review* author predicted that, as work became easier and more machine based, people would look to leisure to give their lives meaning and satisfaction.

Now it is the twenty-first century, and we can see how this future of leisure and freedom from work has materialized. While horrific working conditions and slave labor continue unchecked in far too many countries, here in the United States the people with the most leisure are young men, ages 22–30, who have no college education and have not worked in twelve months. One in five young males are idle, with no prospects for work, marriage, or independent lives (they tend to live with parents or close relatives). And what are they doing with all this time on their hands? You knew it: video games. And in self-reports, they appear to be happy with this life.

We should all be scared.

I recall a conversation with a college professor in his thirties who taught the design of video games at a technical training institute. He taught during the day and then stayed up most nights gaming—a fairly typical life for gamers. I couldn't help myself and raised the issue of real life, that the problem with games was that people got lost in virtual reality and weren't available for the real world. Somehow we got onto the topic of civic responsibility and an upcoming local election. When I asked him if he was paying attention to politics and if he was going to vote, he instantly and proudly replied, "I'm very involved. I'm mayor of my virtual community."

What more is there to say?

We cannot push aside the real world or would we want to. The work that needs doing is rich in meaning and purpose. In my experience, people who notice what's going on would rather be engaged than withdraw. But we have to amend the definition of meaningful. It is still work that makes a difference: But what is the difference we can make?

If it's not creating change at the large scale, if it's not striving to reintroduce sane decision making into large systems, if it doesn't stop the disintegration, then what does it mean to make a difference?

——

I have sat with this question for years, and I haven't found an answer that stops the niggling voice of "Yes, but surely you can think of something with more impact. . . ." The simple answer is found in all philosophies and spiritual traditions: Focus on serving others. Serve individuals; serve small groups; serve an entire community or organization. No matter what is going on around us, we can attend to the people in front of us, to the issues confronting us and there, we offer what we can. We can offer insight and compassion. We can be present. We can stay and not flee. We can be exemplars of the best human qualities. That is a life well lived, even if we didn't save the world.

I've dubbed this the Mother, now Saint, Teresa way of engaging. Before she became an institution with all of its dilemmas, she felt called by God to go into the streets of Calcutta to aid "the unwanted, the unloved, the uncared for." She found the dying and offered them her presence. She wasn't trying to solve the greater problem of why people were dying on the streets; she simply wanted to give them a better death in the company of love. In later life, she willingly went into places of great suffering, in countries torn by war, to rescue children. If she were alive today, I wonder which refugee camps she would be in.

She, like all humanitarians, focused on the victims, not the causes. She sought to relieve suffering, not to eradicate it.

———

This is good work. And it is work that others are eager to do with us. Over many years, I have found more than enough people who want to contribute, to fully engage in solving problems that affect them or that they care about. Or that help relieve the suffering of others. We don't need to motivate them to join with us—we just need to invite them.

In this time of rising insanity and brutality, work that engages our better human qualities is a gift we can offer to others. This is why we create islands of sanity, so that more of us can experience the gift of doing meaningful work on behalf of others. How wonderful to have the chance to engage together in doing good work, no matter what is going on around us. We are richly blessed.

I'm comfortable with the choices I made, I'm proud of those choices. I can be comfortable with the way I've lived until today. As long as we do our best to live in accordance with our values, we don't have to worry about tomorrow because today is enough.

Edward Snowden[8]

WHO DO WE CHOOSE TO BE? NOTES

1 "Once people realize that their wealth is being secretly and arbitrarily confiscated and their welfare systematically degraded by underhanded rulers, the social contact is broken, with possible revolutionary consequences." Keynes describes at length the *arbitrary confiscation* of wealth into the hands of governments and elites as a consequence of inflationary policies (Keynes's italics). This destabilizes the very basis of relationships necessary for capitalism. As disorder and distrust increase, the "process of wealth-getting degenerates into a gamble and a lottery." Quotes from William Ophuls, *Immoderate Greatness*, pp. 60–61. I would note that this attitude seems evident in tech-generation entrepreneurs who approach getting rich as a crap shoot.

2 An ancient Tibetan prophecy, relayed by many Tibetan Buddhist teachers. Joanna Macy, who has spent her lifetime teaching deep ecology and insisting on eco-activism, grounds her work in this prophecy, given to her by her teacher. See www.joannamacy.net.

3 *The Universe in a Single Atom*, His Holiness the Dalai Lama, p. 200. He was addressing decision making in regard to genetics research. I use these with all leaders.

4 Their oral tradition dates the founding as 1142, following a solar eclipse. The founders were two men and one woman (Hiawatha). The "Great League of Peace" brought together five tribal nations; a sixth was added in 1722. Their constitution influenced the U.S. Constitution written in 1789. The Confederation split during the American Revolution; four of the six Iroquois nations sided with the British. George Washington ordered a scorched earth campaign against these four tribes in upper New York State. Refugees fled to Canada.

5 "Uber Begins Its Endgame: Replacing Humans," http://motherboard.vice.com/read/uber-begins-its-endgame-replacing-humans.

6 See Dan Lyons, "Congratulations! You've Been Fired," nytimes.com, April 17, 2016. This article is well worth reading to observe the adolescent cultures at a number of tech companies. "At HubSpot, the software company where I worked for almost two years, when you got fired, it was called 'graduation.' We all would get a cheery email from the boss saying, 'Team, just letting you know that X has graduated and we're all excited to see how she uses her superpowers in her next big adventure.'"

7 Derek Thompson, "The Free Time Paradox in America," theatlantic.com, September 13, 2016, http://www.theatlantic.com/business/archive/2016/09/the-free-time-paradox-in-america.

8 Live-streamed into a conference on mass surveillance held in the Netherlands, November 10, 2016; see https://www.youtube.com/watch?v=98eabjjAEz8&spfreload=10. I recommend watching Snowden's thoughtful responses to questions—a true warrior.

8. NO MATTER WHAT

___

Because they trust themselves they have no need to convince others by deception. Since their confidence has never deteriorated, they need not be fearful of others.

— *Chögyam Trungpa*, Buddhist teacher

Unshakable Confidence, Unquestioned Humility

There have been a few times in this book when I've linked together concepts that may have felt strange, such as when I paired the leaders of social change movements and terrorists. In this essay, I believe it is essential to link confidence with humility. But it may take some explaining.

Confidence, in our deranged identity-manipulating world, has deteriorated into entire industries designed to pump us up with slogans, posters, coffee mugs, cards, even billboards in the United States. We're supposed to believe that we can be anything we want—the greatest, the fittest, the smartest, the fastest—need I go on? And we're supposed to tell everyone about it—all the time. This is hype and self-promotion, not confidence. In fact, it works in the obverse: the less confidence we have, the more we brag about ourselves. This dynamic has been well entrenched in human behavior for eons, but social media has raised it to an art form.

Hype has stolen the true meaning of confidence. In early usage, from the Latin, it meant to have "full trust." And the full was emphasized, "con." When we speak of unshakable confidence, this is close to its original meaning. And what is it that we can trust so fully? Only ourselves.

We can't trust ourselves to be perfect; we can't trust ourselves to be the best at anything; we can't trust ourselves to succeed; we can't trust ourselves to never cause harm and hurt. What we can trust is our disciplined effort to get to know ourselves. We can learn to know our triggers, our habitual reactions, our strengths and weaknesses. All of this is possible—and essential—if we are to lead sanely in the midst of falling-apart craziness.

What I'm about to say here should, by now, feel familiar: We see the world through powerful filters of self. The more we know our filters, the more we can see beyond them. As we get a richer glimpse of our environment, we can respond more intelligently. Intelligence is what gives everything alive the prospect of healthy survival.

The more we know ourselves—how we filter and react to the world—the more trustworthy we can become. It's been said thousands of times, in all faiths and philosophies. Know thyself. What may be less clear in these wise expressions is the reason we learn to know ourselves: we develop a knowledge of self so that we can give up the self and serve others.

—

The distinction between self-help and self-knowledge is important. There are thousands of self-help methods available to design a better you. But here, we aspire to high levels of self-awareness, not to help ourselves but to learn to trust ourselves in difficult situations.

—

We learn to know situations that trigger our aggression; we learn to recognize fear and anxiety when they arise; we learn to recognize when we're relying on hope and fear rather than right action; we learn to notice judgments as they appear. Our motivation is to be more in control of ourselves so that we don't get in the way, and don't give ourselves away, as we work in service to others.

We are not trying to change ourselves; we're not trying to fix anything. Rather, we get curious about who we are, how our mind works. We practice to remove the obstacles that cover up our basic goodness, the fine qualities of being that humans never lose. As we come to know ourselves, without fixing anything, these better qualities surface on their own: We are calmer, more present, more compassionate, more awake, more light-hearted. People enjoy being around us and we enjoy being with them.

Humility is a natural consequence of getting to know ourselves. Yes, we are basically good, but as you see what's in your mind, all sorts of shit surfaces. (Sorry, I can't say that any other way because this is what it always feels like.) In the warrior training I lead, our most popular slogan is "First, be friendly to yourself." If we can't be compassionate to ourselves, there's no chance we can be genuinely compassionate to others. Compassion has to begin at home.

———

Self-compassion is not to be confused with self-love of the common self-help variety. We're not trying to pump ourselves up so that we believe in ourselves. We're committed to knowing ourselves so we can benefit others.

———

Yet even with that good intent, the self we encounter is quite painful. We see the harm we've created, the problems we didn't handle well, our unstoppable jealousies, passions, cravings. In other words, when we see all the ways we're being human, it's hard not to beat ourselves up—especially in the West, where self-doubt and self-loathing are our specialty. The challenge is to treat ourselves with as much kindness and love as we offer a good friend who is suffering.[1]

The qualities we extend to a friend in need usually are quite tender and patient (at least at the beginning.) As we learn how to hold ourselves with tenderness, perhaps even with curiosity, we develop a quality of gentleness and acceptance. We accept that we're just like every other human—we try hard; we mess up; we try again; we fail again—this is what it means to live a life. There's no avoiding it—it's just the way things are. Once we know this and truly accept it, we can't help but be gentled. And it is this gentle quality, arising from true humility, that gives us the confidence to be in the difficult places and do whatever we can for others.

Behind the confidence is always gentleness. Behind the gentleness is always confidence.

No Hope No Fear

I have been encouraging people to explore the place beyond hope and fear for more than two decades.[2] (Seems to be what I most need to learn.) Because I always bring it up to audiences, I've learned that it's the hottest hot button among us activists. Hope is the bedrock motivator for our work. It doesn't matter how many inspiring quotes from heroic people I present, or the logic behind the advice to abandon hope. My experience is that we think that the opposite of hope is despair, and because we so desperately want to be of service and maintain our strength and energy, we do everything we can to avoid falling into the abyss of despair. We cling to hope to prevent the fall.

This is a place I am intimately familiar with—the abyss of despair. Sometimes I notice early on that I'm walking toward that edge and can keep myself from getting any closer. Other times, when I'm overcome by bad news from the world or from a friend, quite suddenly I notice that my toes already are curled over the edge. I feel trapped with nowhere to run. Nowhere to hide. No exit. I just want to scream my outrage into the black silence.

I have learned from these frequent times at the edge that I don't need to cheer myself up or inflate myself with optimism and resolve. I don't need to ignore my emotions and just get back to work. I need to accept where I am and just stay there for a while. I'm not going to jump and I'm not going to turn away. I'm going to find my ground right here, staring into this darkness. And slowly, without hope, without fear, clarity begins to dawn. This is what is. I know who I aspire to be. I know what to do. Let's get on with doing what I can, where I am, with those who are with me.

Long ago I realized that efforts to stay hopeful are a waste of time and energy. Hope is not an innocent motivator. It's bipolar: fear is its other nature. Every time we get lifted up by a hoped-for outcome, we get dragged down when we don't succeed. Hope then fear. The endless cycle.

———

Hope is a filter we willingly place on reality. Instead of noticing what is, we obscure it with our needs and dreams, with our egos. Sometimes we do things because that's the best action possible; sometimes we do things so people will notice us. "Don't expect applause," my teacher told me. When I don't, I notice the world beyond what I want it to be, free of me, free of hope and fear.

When we move beyond the filters of what we hope for, we can see what needs to be done—right action—and act appropriately. We can act with compassion and insight.

Think about your personal experiences with the place beyond hope and fear. I'm certain there've been many times when you found yourself stepping forward without hesitation. Something in the situation called you into spontaneous action without calculating costs and benefits. This is the definition of courage—actions that spring from an open heart without premeditation. (The word *courage* comes from the old French word for "heart.") Sometimes these spontaneous actions are good; sometimes they get us into a lot of trouble; sometimes people lose their lives rushing in to save others. What's important to notice in your experience is how it felt to be fearless. You were also hopeless. You did what had to be done as it appeared in that moment. You weren't thinking of outcomes, and you had more than enough energy.

There are many other circumstances when you may have experienced the place beyond hope and fear. I've witnessed it in leaders who have struggled and struggled to please a boss, a board, a politician. At some point, it becomes obvious that there's no way they will get approval and/or funding for the outcomes they need. The opposition will not yield. At this point, they give up hope and just do the work.

There was one year when Angela Blanchard was hit with a barrage of attacks from external critics, people who questioned (and even denied) everything her organization had accomplished, who slandered her personally—it was a very ugly year. This sent her into depression and withdrawal. From that dark night, Angela arose with clarity and renewed energy. Their attacks didn't matter. She knew Neighborhood Centers Inc. was doing the right work. Even if the attacks took hold and they lost funding, they were going to continue as before. She coined their mantra: "We do good work because we do good work."

That's the place beyond hope and fear. And you already know this place.

Hope is not the conviction that something will turn out well, but the certainty that something is worth doing no matter how it turns out.

Václav Havel, Czech leader

Making Our Shoulders Strong

For many years, leaders were preoccupied with the idea of legacy. This was the era when we were all incredibly optimistic about the changes we were creating. Well-led organizations offered direct evidence of positive changes that resulted from working with the new paradigm of living systems. It was natural for leaders to want the value they had created to continue into the future beyond their individual tenure. These days, I don't hear legacy talked about nearly as much—conversations tend to focus on just keeping things afloat, surviving the present craziness with one's integrity still recognizable.

Legacy is an important thing to reflect on at the end of a long and fruitful career. What had been built was of real value; it needs to be sustained independent of a change in leadership. A body of work that has been carefully crafted deserves to endure beyond the life of the creator. Having persevered to the end, the leader, artist, parent, citizen should be remembered for their contribution. And their work should live on, supporting those who pick up the torch and continue the work.

Over many years, I watched as the work of fine corporate and political leaders—work based on ethical, humane values, that had led to extraordinary results and very grateful staff—I saw this good work vanish. Nearly overnight. "The King is dead. Long live the King!" In corporations, time after time I saw that new leaders behaved like male lions who move in on a new pride and kill all the cubs of the prior lion-lord. I soon realized that this is how it usually is: raw ego power destroys what has been so lovingly crafted by wise leaders. Leaving a legacy in an organization

always runs the risk of being destroyed by needs for power that supersede any interest in sanity.

Yet there is a great need to leave a legacy, because we have been blessed to walk in the footsteps and stand on the shoulders of those who went before us. We do not spring fresh upon the scene as a superhero, newborn and powerful, ready to solve all problems. This *is* the behavior of several tech billionaires who, with compassionate hearts and unfathomable sums of money, believe they can apply their wealth and technology to solve everything. The Chan-Zuckerberg Initiative (of Facebook wealth), in September 2016 announced a $3 billion project, "to cure, prevent or manage all diseases by the end of the century." Beautifully intentioned work—based on the belief that science and computer programming can solve all the problems of humanity.[3] The Progress Trap.

What is legacy, then, if not changing things, if not making life better in the future? What is the difference we've made that we want to offer to future generations?

You are the result of the love of thousands.

Linda Hogan, Native American Chickasaw

What Do You Want to Be Remembered For?

I believe you know the answer to this question, and, if not, think again about those who willingly offered you their shoulders. Perhaps they didn't know that for all these years you've relied on their example and taken strength from them. Probably they have no idea of how often you think of them, how you view their lives now that you're older. I expect they'd be shocked to learn that they've served this role in your life, that they left a legacy.

If I could have a conversation now with my deceased parents and grandparents (which I dearly long for), I would reflect back to them how much their examples have grounded me, how often I draw upon their qualities, how much I love them for their struggles and perseverance to give me my good life. If I could have this conversation, I know they would be surprised more than honored. They just did what needed to be done, with what they had, in a culture whose values were clear and commonly shared.

My English grandparents raised five children in poverty in World War I and then endured World War II, in which several of the siblings served. My grandfather had served in the Boer War in South Africa and suffered from PTSD, but that was not a known condition then (and you just got on with life). Although their lives were extremely difficult living with the horrors and losses of twentieth-century world wars, they persevered, as did most people of that time. Through my father, I felt their influence. I was raised with the classic English values of honesty, duty, discipline, and "stiff upper lip." There is work to be done—just get on with it without complaint. (There were so many times when I tried this with my own children as teens, but.... However, now that they're grown, I see these values in them.)

My maternal grandmother was an early feminist, as were many Edwardian women (e.g., the Suffragettes). She led a full life dedicated to noble causes and always encouraged women to step forward. She was the first woman qualified for the Rabbinate, studied education with John Dewey, and was one of the first Jewish women to enlist during World War I in the Army Motor Corps. She devoted her life to the cause of Zionism (I know she would be heartbroken today as she had sponsored Arab-Jewish programs and policies, and inclusion of Palestinians), including running for Congress in New York City in 1948 to bring attention to her causes. She joined a kibbutz in the 1930s after losing heart with large-scale organizing, and contributed daily physical labor as well as writing. In the 1920s, she was the third president of Hadassah, the national Jewish women's organization. She traveled frequently to the United States, speaking, fund-raising, and to be with her family. She died when I was 35, so I grew up with her guidance and insistence on a life of service as a woman leader. (I also recall that at age 5 or 6 she told me I should be a writer.)

Obviously, I stand on very strong shoulders from my grandparents. It was very good to bring them here, and now I'd ask you: Who are the people in your life that you depend on as ground and support for your life? Particularly, as I've already asked, who were the warriors in your life? And how might they support you now as you step forward into this role of Warrior for the Human Spirit?

My personal aspiration for legacy simplifies with age. I want to leave behind strong shoulders. Shoulders strong enough for some to stand on to carry them forward into whatever awaits. After a lifetime of yearning to change things on a large scale, this simple aspiration now feels more than enough.

Sir Isaac Newton, before he died, wrote this about his work:
"I don't know what I may seem to
the world, but, as to myself,
I seem to have been only like a boy
playing on the sea-shore,
and diverting myself in now and then
finding a smoother pebble or
a prettier shell than ordinary,
whilst the great ocean of truth lay
all undiscovered before me."

NO MATTER WHAT: NOTES

[1] If you're intrigued by this possibility, see Recommended Readings for books that teach how to extend genuine loving kindness toward yourself.

[2] This theme appears in my work more than any other. For example: two DVDs, *Eight Fearless Questions*; *Perseverance*. Books: *So Far from Home*. Article, "The Place Beyond Fear and Hope," http://margaretwheatley.com/wpcontent/uploads/2014/12/BeyondHopeandFear.pdf.

[3] In 2015, on the birth of their daughter, Mark Zuckerberg and his wife created the Chan-Zuckerberg Initiative and vowed to devote 99 percent of their wealth (about $45 billion) to create "a world where our generation can advance human potential and promote equality for all children in the next generation." Its initial areas of focus will be personalized learning, curing disease, connecting people, building strong communities, reducing poverty, providing equal rights and spreading understanding across nations, and harnessing clean energy.

CODA

—

When There Is No Reality

CODA

At the end of 2016, following the U.S. election, it became clear that the Internet played a very significant influence over the news that people received about issues and candidates, supposedly information used to determine their vote. We learned of incendiary websites created in Eastern Europe by young people to make money; of bots (robots) programmed to phone millions with lies and misinformation. We learned that nearly half of Americans got their news from Facebook (for Millennials, it was over 60 percent) and that those news feeds did not distinguish between what came from actual newsrooms or from friends. What was fake news, what was real? Did it matter?

The term *echo chamber* became popular to describe how we are fed "news" that we like, from people we like, determined by algorithms on Facebook and Google too complex for any one person to understand.[1] Personal interests and preferences solidify into narrow, rock-hard positions as we are fed only news that we like. Facebook research had already proven that if we receive news that pleases us, happy emotions cause us to buy more things advertised online.

It will never be known how much influence this manufactured environment of willful distortions had on the election or what will happen in future elections in the United States and other countries, or to public interest in government behavior and policy decisions. But one thing is clear: we are witnessing the death of reality.

As a Buddhist, I've spent long years training my mind to not be deceived by appearances, to experience the illusory nature of everything. I was taught early on that nothing is what I think it is. Nothing that appears is its own independent self. What appears to be solid will soon be gone. Everything changes.

But this is different. We cannot live in this world without a commonly shared sense of what is important, what is of value, what is "real." The Internet has enabled global groundlessness unparalleled in human history because of its scale and penetration.[2]

Our senses are bombarded with lies, rumors, conspiracies, out of which we make sense according to which group we choose to affiliate with. How do we make sense of the larger world beyond our group? We don't. We contract inward, we seek self-protection, and the world becomes ever more hostile and frightening.

And then, as is true throughout history, someone comes along and gives our battered selves something to hold onto. His promises do not need to be based on reality; they don't have to make sense. They only need to offer people the prospect of relief from fear. In a world so wildly out of control, people are promised a place to ground. And others are here, just like me, who've found the same ground. Nothing else matters. Here is where we can feel secure. Here we will be taken care of. Here we feel rescued from the awful chaos.

Humans cannot live without meaning. The greater the uncertainty, the more our desperate grasp for a handhold, a shred of meaning. Is our meaning found in the realization that we are the chosen ones? The realization that everyone else is inferior? The hope that our former way of life will be restored? The promise that someone will end the sickening fear and noise in our heads?

When there is no shared reality and people are flailing for ground, whoever declares a reality that promises to reduce fear becomes the leader. It is always this way, and this is where we are now.

This is the reality that summons us to be Warriors for the Human Spirit.

Humans have a responsibility to find themselves where they are, in their own proper time and place, in the history to which they belong and to which they must inevitably contribute either their response or their evasions, either truth and act, or mere slogan and gesture.

Thomas Merton, Catholic monk, author, activist

CODA: NOTES

[1] See Kartenk Hosanagar, "Blame the Echo Chamber on Facebook, but Blame Yourself Too," wired.com, November 25, 2016; and David Lee, "Facebook Fake News Row: Mark Zuckerberg Is a Politician Now," bbc.com, November 19, 2016. I'm sure there's been much more written since then.

[2] "Truth and Lies in the Age of Trump" by The Editorial Board, nytimes.com, December 12, 2016.

The Warriors arise
when the people need protection

The human spirit needs protection

May the Warriors arise

APPENDIX

The Six Ages of a Civilization's Growth and Collapse
as described by Sir John Glubb

"The life-expectation of a great nation, it appears, commences with a violent, and usually unforeseen, outburst of energy, and ends in a lowering of moral standards, cynicism, pessimism and frivolity."[1]

Glubb studied thirteen empires in the Middle East, Asia, and Europe (where he had served as a military commander), from Assyria in 859 BCE to modern Britain in 1950. The pattern of the decline and fall of these superpowers was startlingly clear. It didn't matter where they were or what technology they had or how they exercised power. They all declined in the same stages, and it always took ten generations, about 250 years. The logic of this is very clear: Each generation matures in better socioeconomic circumstances that have been created for them by the preceding generation. Thus, there is always a march to increasing materialism. In every generation, youth will have higher expectations for comfort than their parents. Improved material conditions create attitudinal changes that insist on still more material changes and, predictably, because of this wealth and erosion of morality, the civilization declines into decadence.

1. Age of Pioneers. New pioneers or conquerors are usually poor, hardy, enterprising, and aggressive. They seem to appear from nowhere, surprising the dominant civilization. They possess fearless initiative, energy, and courage. The decaying empire that they overthrow is wealthy but defensive-minded. Pioneers are practical and experimental; action is their solution to every problem. They have strong virtues: optimism, confidence, devotion to duty, a sense of honor, shared purpose, and a strict moral code.

2. Age of Conquest. Conquerors adopt the military ways of the empire they have conquered. They are more organized, disciplined, and professional in their military campaigns. They have strong codes of glory and honor, often with a religious basis that calls for heroic self-sacrifice; for example, the terrorizing Genghis Kahn (thirteenth century) said that God had delegated him to exterminate the decadent races of the civilized world.

3. Age of Commerce. There is enough pride to support a great military that guards the borders, but gradually the desire to make money gains hold of the public. The first half is "peculiarly splendid. The nation is proud, united and full of self-confidence." There is still some sense of personal honor as men search for new forms of wealth in profitable enterprises in the far corners of the Earth. But then, wealth pours in; values of glory and honor dissipate as core values become the bottom line and the size of your bank account. The wealthy business community spends some of its money on splendid buildings, palaces, communications, roads, hotels, railways—according to the varied needs of the ages.

4. Age of Affluence. Change is from service to selfishness. Gradually "the Age of Affluence silences the voice of duty. The object of the young and the ambitious is no longer fame, honor or service, but cash." Education changes from learning to qualifications for high salaried jobs. At the end of the eleventh century, as Arab power was declining, the moralist Ghazali complained, "Students no longer attend college to acquire learning and virtue, but to obtain those qualifications which will enable them to grow rich." There is still enough patriotism to have military defending its frontiers, but greed replaces duty and public service.

Wealth dazzles outsiders. Defensiveness spreads. Great walls are built. "Money being in better supply than courage, subsidies instead of weapons are employed to buy off enemies." Economics is used to control and pacify. "History seems to indicate that great nations do not normally disarm from motives of conscience, but owing to the weakening of a sense of duty in the citizens, and the increase of selfishness and the desire for wealth and ease."

5. The Age of Intellect

a. The arts and knowledge expand in every period of decline, in every empire. Merchant princes endow the arts and also start colleges. For example, in eleventh-century Arabia, the Sultan Malik Shah built a university in every town. Classical Chinese political thought emerged during the worst of the breakdown. The Warring States period (~421–222 BCE) produced some of China's major philosophical, literary, and scientific achievements, including Confucius and Sun Tzu.[2]

b. Natural sciences advance. In the ninth century, Arabs measured the circumference of the Earth with remarkable accuracy, 700 years before the West discovered the Earth was not flat. Yet the Arab empire collapsed less than 50 years later.

c. Intellectuals flourish and often serve illiterate rulers. Intellectualism leads to endless and incessant talking. "Thus public affairs drift from bad to worse, amid an unceasing cacophony of argument. … Amid a Babel of talk, the ship drifts on to the rocks."

d. The human intellect can solve all problems. It is assumed that any situation can be saved by mental cleverness, with no need for altruism or dedication to a cause. "The brilliant but cynical intellectual appears at the opposite end of the spectrum from the emotional self-sacrifice of the hero or the martyr. Yet there are times when the perhaps unsophisticated self-dedication of the hero is more essential than the sarcasms of the clever."

e. Civil dissensions intensify. In times of national decline, internal political hatreds increase, even as the survival of the nation becomes precarious. Political factions don't stop their rivalries, even to save their country. The weakening empire of Byzantium in the fourteenth century was threatened, and indeed dominated, by the Ottoman Turks. Yet instead of pulling together, the Byzantines spent the last fifty years of their history fighting one another in repeated civil wars, until the Ottomans moved in and administered the final blow.

Another source of civil division is created by the influx of foreigners drawn irresistibly to the imperial wealth and glory, creating a polyglot population that no longer shares the same values. Intellectual discourse has led to a society that is increasingly "value-free," no longer believing in much of anything or taking anything seriously. The original spirit, the moral core, the founding ideals of the civilization are no longer present in its diverse population.

6. The Age of Decadence

After too long a period of wealth and power, empires decline in identical ways. "Frivolity, aestheticism, hedonism, cynicism, pessimism, narcissism, consumerism, materialism, nihilism, fatalism, fanaticism and other negative behaviors and attitudes suffuse the population. Politics is increasingly corrupt, life increasingly unjust. A cabal of insiders accrues wealth and power at the expense of the citizenry, fostering a fatal opposition of interests between haves and have nots. The majority lives for bread and circuses; worships celebrities instead of divinities . . . throws off social and moral restraints, especially on sexuality; shirks duties but insists on entitlements."[3]

The Roman mob demanded free meals and public games, passionate about gladiatorial shows, chariot races, and athletic events. In the Byzantine Empire, the rivalries of the Greens and the Blues in the Hippodrome attained the importance of a major crisis.

Declining nations have celebrity cultures: athletes, singers, actors.

Belief in one's eternal greatness emerges. The wealthy leaders believe they will always be leaders of mankind, so they relax their energies, and spend an increasing part of their time in leisure, amusement or sport. The illusion of superiority causes them to employ cheap foreign labor or slaves to engage in menial tasks. These poorer peoples are only too happy to migrate to the wealthy cities of the empire, and thus dilute the homogeneous character and original shared values of the conquering peoples.

The beneficent or welfare state appears. As long as it retains its status of leadership, the imperial people are glad to be generous, even if slightly condescending.

The rights of citizenship are generously bestowed on every race, even those formerly subjugated, and the equality of mankind is proclaimed. The Roman Empire passed through this phase, when equal citizenship was thrown open to all peoples, as did the Arab Empire of Baghdad. State assistance to the young and the poor was equally generous. University students received government grants to cover their expenses while they were receiving higher education. The state likewise offered free medical treatment to the poor. Free public hospitals sprang up all over the Arab world from Spain to what is now Pakistan in the ninth century. "The impression that it will always be automatically rich causes the declining empire to spend lavishly on its own benevolence, until such time as the economy collapses, the universities are closed and the hospitals fall into ruin."

7. Religion

After the empire has fallen, when money no longer rules everything, religion regains its sway and a new era begins. But only after the fall.

As the Arab Empire Was Collapsing: Baghdad in 861 CE

Sir John Glubb

In the first half of the ninth century, Baghdad enjoyed its High Noon as the greatest and the richest city in the world. In 861, however, the reigning Khalif (caliph), Mutawakkil, was murdered by his Turkish mercenaries, who set up a military dictatorship, which lasted for some thirty years. During this period the empire fell apart.

The works of the contemporary historians of Baghdad in the early tenth century are still available. They deeply deplored the degeneracy of the times in which they lived, emphasizing particularly the indifference to religion, the increasing materialism and the laxity of sexual morals. They lamented also the corruption of the officials of the government and the fact that politicians always seemed to amass large fortunes while they were in office. The historians commented bitterly on the extraordinary influence acquired by popular singers over young people, resulting in a decline in sexual morality. The 'pop' singers of Baghdad accompanied their erotic songs on the lute, an instrument resembling the modern guitar. In the second half of the tenth century, as a result, much obscene sexual language came increasingly into use, such as would not have been tolerated in an earlier age. Several khalifs issued orders banning 'pop' singers from the capital, but within a few years they always returned.

An increase in the influence of women in public life has often been associated with national decline. The later Romans complained that, although Rome ruled the world, women ruled Rome. In the tenth century, a similar tendency was observable in the Arab Empire, the women demanding admission to the professions hitherto monopolized by men. "What," wrote the contemporary historian, Ibn Bessam, "have the professions of clerk, tax-collector or preacher to do with women? These occupations have always been limited to men alone." Many women practiced law, while others obtained posts as university professors. There was an agitation for the appointment of female judges, which, however, does not appear to have succeeded. Soon after this period, government and public order collapsed, and foreign invaders overran the country. The resulting increase in confusion and violence made it unsafe for women to move unescorted in the streets, with the result that this feminist movement collapsed.

Author: John Bagot Glubb was born in 1897. He served throughout World War I in France and Belgium, being wounded three times and awarded the Military Cross. In 1920 he volunteered for service in Iraq, as a regular officer, but in 1926 resigned his commission and accepted an administrative post under the Iraq government. In 1930, however, he signed a contract to serve the Transjordan government (now Jordan). From 1939 to 1956 he commanded the famous Jordan Arab Legion, which was in reality the Jordan Army. He published seventeen books, chiefly on the Middle East, and lectured widely in Britain, the United States, and Europe.

Source: http://people.uncw.edu/kozloffm/glubb.pdf.

Primary Descriptors of the Collapse of Complex Societies

from Joseph Tainter

Joseph Tainter defines collapse as primarily a political phenomenon with consequences in all other spheres such as economics, art, and culture. *"A society has collapsed when it displays a rapid, significant loss of an established level of sociopolitical complexity."*

The complexity has developed over many generations; eventually it becomes so cumbersome and expensive that the society can no longer maintain what it has created. Collapse happens quickly, within a few decades, marked by a significant loss of sociopolitical structures.

Collapse is manifest in such things as[4]

- A lower degree of stratification and social differentiation;
- Less economic and occupational specialization, of individuals, groups, and territories;
- Less centralized control; that is, less regulation and integration of diverse economic and political groups by elites;
- Less behavioral control and regimentation;
- Less investment in the epiphenomena of complexity, those elements that define the concept of "civilization": monumental architecture, artistic and literary achievements, and the like;
- Less flow of information between individuals, between political and economic groups, and between a center and its periphery;
- Less sharing, trading, and redistribution of resources;
- Less overall coordination and organization of individuals and groups;
- A smaller territory integrated within a single political entity.

APPENDIX: NOTES

[1] Except where otherwise noted, quoted passages are from Sir John Glubb, *The Fate of Empires and Search for Survival* (1976), http://people.uncw.edu/kozloffm/glubb.pdf.

[2] Tainter, Kindle Locations 187–189.

[3] Ophuls, *Immoderate Greatness*, p. 49.

[4] Joseph A. Tainter, *The Collapse of Complex Societies* (New Studies in Archaeology), Kindle Location 147.

RECOMMENDED READINGS

Each book listed here is one that I truly value. Some are old friends; some are new discoveries. But each author presents views and perspectives that are fresh, brilliant, and outside the norm, which of course is my favorite place to dwell. I hope you enjoy these treasures.

ANTHROPOLOGY

Davis, Wade. *The Wayfinders: Why Ancient Wisdom Matters in the Modern World*. Toronto: House of Anansi Press, 2009. Also available in audio from CBC Massey Lecture Series, the source of the book. http://www.cbc.ca/radio/ideas/the-2009-cbc-massey-lectures-the-wayfinders-why-ancient-wisdom-matters-in-the-modern-world-1.2946883

Hancock, Graham. *Magicians of the Gods: The Forgotten Wisdom of Earth's Lost Civilization*. London: Coronet Books, 2015.

Stringer, Chris. *Lone Survivors: How We Came to Be the Only Humans on Earth*. New York: Times Books/Holt, 2012.

COLLAPSE

Chödrön, Pema. *When Things Fall Apart*. Boulder, CO: Shambhala Publications, 2016.

Glubb, John. *The Fate of Empires and Search for Survival*. 1976. http://people.uncw.edu/kozloffm/glubb.pdf

Ophuls, William. *Immoderate Greatness: Why Civilizations Fail*. CreateSpace, 2012.

———. *Plato's Revenge: Politics in the Age of Ecology*. Cambridge, MA: MIT Press, 2013.

Tainter, Joseph. *The Collapse of Complex Societies*. Cambridge: Cambridge University Press, 1988.

Wright, Ronald. *A Short History of Progress*. Carroll and Graf Publishers, 2005. Also available from CBC Massey Lecture Series, the source of the book. http://www.cbc.ca/radio/ideas/the-2004-cbc-massey-lectures-a-short-history-of-progress-1.2946872

INTERNET

Carr, Nicholas. *The Glass Cage: Automation and Us*. New York: Norton, 2015.

———. *The Shallows: What the Internet Is Doing to Our Brains*. New York: Norton, 2011.

———. *Utopia Is Creepy: And Other Provocations*. New York: Norton, 2016.

RECOMMENDED READINGS

Kardaras, Nicholas. *Glow Kids: How Screen Addiction Is Hijacking Our Kids—and How to Break the Trance.* New York: St. Martin's, 2016.

MEDITATION

Salzberg, Sharon. *Loving Kindness: The Revolutionary Art of Happiness.* Boulder, CO: Shambhala Publications, 2002

———. *Real Happiness: The Power of Meditation: A 28 Day Program.* New York: Workman Publishing, 2011.

———. *Real Happiness at Work: Meditations for Accomplishment, Achievement, and Peace.* New York: Workman Publishing, 2013.

Trungpa, Chögyam, and Carolyn Rose Gimian. *Mindfulness in Action: Making Friends with Yourself through Meditation and Everyday Awareness.* Boulder, CO: Shambhala Publications, 2015.

Wallace, Alan. *Mind in the Balance: Meditation in Science, Buddhism, and Christianity.* New York: Columbia University Press, 2009.

SCIENCE

Geology

Childs, Craig. *Apocalyptic Planet: Field Guide to the Ever-ending Earth.* New York: Pantheon, 2012.

Living Systems

Capra, Fritjof, and Pier Luigi Luisi. *The Systems View of Life: A Unifying Vision.* Cambridge: Cambridge University Press, 2014

Capra, Fritjof, and Ugo Mattei. *The Ecology of Law: Toward a Legal System in Tune with Nature and Community.* Oakland, CA: Berrett-Koehler, 2015.

Margulis, Lynn. *Symbiotic Planet: A New Look at Evolution.* New York: Basic Books, 1998.

Philosophy of Science and/or Technology

Ellul, Jacques. *Perspectives on Our Age: Jacques Ellul Speaks on His Life and Work.* Toronto: House of Anansi, 2004.

Kuhn, Thomas. *The Structure of Scientific Revolutions* (2nd ed.). Chicago: University of Chicago Press, 1970.

Physics

The Dalai Lama. *The Universe in a Single Atom: The Convergence of Science and Spirituality*. New York: Three Rivers Press, 2005.

Gribbin, John. *The Quantum Mystery*. A Kindle Single, 2015.

Musser, George. *Spooky Action at a Distance: The Phenomenon That Reimagines Space and Time*. New York: Scientific American/ Farrar, Straus and Giroux, 2016.

Ricard, Matthieu, and Trinh Xuan Thuan. *The Quantum and the Lotus: A Journey to the Frontiers Where Science and Buddhism Meet*. New York: Three Rivers Press, 2004.

SOCIAL COMMENTARY

Mann, Michael, and Tom Toles. *The Madhouse Effect: How Climate Change Denial Is Threatening Our Planet, Destroying Our Politics, and Driving Us Crazy*. New York: Columbia University Press, 2016.

Gray, John. *The Silence of Animals: On Progress and Other Modern Myths*. New York: Farrar, Straus and Giroux, 2014.

———. *The Soul of the Marionette: A Short Inquiry into Human Freedom*. New York: Farrar, Straus and Giroux, 2015.

WARRIORSHIP

Frankl, Victor. *Man's Search for Meaning*. New York: Beacon, 2015 (New Gift Edition of original with added material).

Funk, Mary Margaret, OSB. *Humility Matters: Toward Purity of Heart*. Collegeville, MN: Liturgical Press, 2013.

Gimian, James, and Barry Boyce. *The Rules of Victory: How to Transform Chaos and Conflict-Strategies from the Art of War*. Boulder, CO: Shambhala Publications, 2008.

Kahane, Adam. *Power and Love: A Theory and Practice of Social Change*. San Francisco: Berrett-Koehler, 2010.

Mandela, Nelson. *Long Walk to Freedom: The Autobiography of Nelson Mandela*. New York: Little, Brown, 2008.

McCarthy, Margaret Cain, and Mary Ann Zollmann, eds. *Power of Sisterhood: Women Religious Tell the Story of the Apostolic Visitation*. Lanham, MD: University Press of America, 2014.

Palmer, Parker. *The Active Life: A Spirituality of Work, Creativity and Caring*. New York: HarperCollins, 1990.

ACKNOWLEDGMENTS

Blessed with so many friends, advisors, teachers, and family, without naming you individually, I offer my boundless gratitude and love.

For all who read my books and put these ideas into practice, I thank you. Your support, encouragement, and experimentation are essential to me. If you didn't let me know of your existence, I wouldn't continue to write and teach.

May we continue to strengthen as a community of brave people intent on discovering how best to serve others so that more people may be creative, generous, and kind as we encounter the gathering darkness.

Sundance, Utah
December 2016

INDEX

INDEX

INDEX

Language, and cultural identity, 68, 96n3
Laws of thermodynamics, 28–29
Leadership
    in crisis, 200–206
    in emergence, 230–232
    ethics of, 80–81
    fear used by, 54, 55
    future focus of, 57–60
    integrity of, 92–95
    in island of sanity, 49, 51–53
    legacy of, 281–285
    manipulating information, 106–107
    in military, 57–60
    as noble profession, 4–5, 8
    of nuns and sisters, 86–95, 202–205
    personal experiences with, 51–52
    sane, 32–33
    in self-organization, 155–165, 167–169
    in social movements, 158–165
    in time of collapse, 48–49, 246–252
Leadership and the New Science (Wheatley), 19, 86, 104
Leadership Conference of Women Religious (LCWR), 86–95
Learning, 116–121
    in After Action Review, 128–132, 197
    and decision making, 124–125
    deep, 118–119, 122
    diverse perspectives in, 197–198
    of living systems, 29, 100, 116
    as machine function, 116–121
    organizational, 124, 129
    in social movements, 160
Lee, Grace (Grace Lee Boggs), 25n1, 159, 162–163, 166
Legacy, 281–285
Leibniz, Gottfried Wilhelm, 174
Leisure time in freedom from work, 267–268
Leroi-Gourhan, Andre, 53
Lewis, John, 159, 171n17
Lewontin, Richard, 173
Life
    beginning of, 64, 96n1
    cognition in, 100
Living systems, 12–13, 15, 28–29
    boundary of, 63, 64, 100
    dynamics of, 230–231
    identity of, 62–97, 142
    information in, 100–102
    interconnectedness in, 212–214
    learning of, 29, 100, 116
    open and closed, 28–29, 64
    self-organizing, 48, 142–143

Love
    compared to fear in organization, 55
    and kindness toward self, 277, 288n1

Machine learning, 116–121
Macy, Joanna, 271n2
Mandela, Nelson, 158, 159, 171n16, 253
Manipulation
    of consumers, 70
    of information, 106–107, 108, 292, 293
Marshall, Stephanie Pace, 200–202, 227
Maturana, Humberto, 174–175
Maudlin, Tim, 219, 242n5
Meaningful work, 267–270
Merton, Thomas, 294
Military operations, 191–192
    After Action Review in, 128–132, 197, 198
    leadership in, 57–60
    risk of death in, 77
    and wars in collapse of complexity, 248
Miller, Henry, 141
Mindfulness, 264, 265
Money as motivator, 54, 56
Motivation, 54–56, 159–160
    hope in, 278, 279
    of terrorists, 97n8
Muir, John, 211
Muller, Wayne, 253
Musk, Elon, 45
Muslims, 149, 150
Musser, George, 217, 242n8
Myth of progress, 31, 38–41

Naming ourselves, 253–256
Native peoples
    ancestral lands of, 224
    cultural traditions of, 236–237
    Great Binding Law of Iroquois, 259
    teen suicide among, 225
    as water protectors at Standing Rock, 79
Neighborhood Centers Inc. (NCI), 238–239, 280
Neural networks, 116, 119, 122
Neurochemicals, 110
Neuroscience, 180, 218
Newton, Isaac, 115, 287
Ng, Andrew, 119, 122
Nhat Hahn, Thich, 243n20
Nobility of leadership, 4–5, 8
Nonlocality, 208n14, 216, 217, 242n8
Nuns and sisters
    in Leadership Conference of Women Religious, 86–95

INDEX

AUTHOR: MARGARET WHEATLEY, Ed.D.

Now in my 70s, I can look back and appreciate what a rich and blessed life I've lived. I've been able to give my curiosity free rein and to be with extraordinary teachers. I've been able to explore a wide range of disciplines and lived in several different cultures. I've learned from an incredible diversity of people, from indigenous peoples to the Dalai Lama, from small town ministers to senior government ministers, from leading scientists to National Park rangers, from engaged activists to solitary monastics. This access to so many sources of experience and wisdom, held in the container of friendship, continues to deepen my resolve to bring whatever I'm learning into my books and teachings. For me, privilege is a responsibility rather than a source of guilt. Having experienced so much, I want to find the best means to communicate with all of you as we aspire to do meaningful work and be of service in this ever-darkening world.

I had an excellent liberal arts education at the University of Rochester and University College London. In the mid-sixties, I spent two years in the Peace Corps in Korea, learning to thrive in a culture totally foreign to me, teaching junior and senior high school English. I received a Master of Arts degree from New York University in Media Ecology with Neil Postman. My doctorate is from Harvard's program in Administration, Planning, and Social Policy, with a focus on organizational behavior and change.

I have been a consultant and speaker since 1973, and have worked with almost all types of organizations and people, on all continents (except Antarctica). Working in so many different places, with all types of people, fed both my curiosity and ability to recognize patterns of behavior common across cultural and institutional differences. And it kept me alert to changing trends in leadership. I am fond of making generalizations, sometimes to the annoyance of others, but they feel genuine and accurate to me because of the scope and depth of my work.

I have served as full-time graduate management faculty at two institutions, Cambridge College in Cambridge, Massachusetts, and The Marriott School of Management, Brigham Young University, Provo, Utah. I've been a formal advisor for leadership programs in England, Croatia, Denmark, Australia and the United States and, in Berkana, with leadership initiatives in India, Senegal, Zimbabwe,

AUTHOR: MARGARET WHEATLEY

South Africa, Mexico, Brazil, Greece, Canada and Europe. Since 2009, I have had a formal appointment (President approved) to serve on the National Parks Advisory Board. My portfolio has focused on leadership and culture change within the system of 400+ parks. This work has been among the most rewarding of my career, because of the mission of National Parks and the dedicated and smart people who work to fulfill this mission under increasingly difficult circumstances.

I am co-founder and president of The Berkana Institute, a global nonprofit founded in 1991. Berkana has been a leader in experimenting with new organizational forms based on a coherent theory of how living systems organize, adapt and change. We've worked in partnership with a rich diversity of people around the world who strengthen their communities by working with the wisdom and wealth already present in their people, traditions and environment. Berkana is now training Warriors for the Human Spirit, leaders who learn-as-community, training with discipline and dedication to develop a stable mind and skillful means. These spiritual warriors do their work with compassion and insight, vowing to refrain from using aggression and fear to accomplish their ends. www.berkana.org.

I've written nine books and nearly 100 articles (downloadable for free on my website). My writings have been an invitation to explore new ways of being and thinking based on wisdom drawn from new science, history, and many spiritual traditions. I've wanted to discover how to apply such rich and crucial wisdom to the challenges of leadership and how to live well together as community, no matter what.

I was raised on the East Coast of the U.S., in New York and then Boston; I've lived in Utah (happily) since 1989. I have two adult sons and have raised five stepchildren, all seven from the same father. There are 21 grandchildren (and counting) and three great-grandchildren. My family, friends and work bring me joy, and so does the time I spend in the true quiet of wilderness or wandering deep in the red rock canyons of Utah.

I enjoy being present through the lens of a camera; all of the photos here are mine and reflect my delight in noticing what's going on.

Margaret J. Wheatley Inc.
P.O. Box 1407, Provo, Utah 84603 Tel: 801-377-2996
info@margaretwheatley.com. www.margaretwheatley.com

Berrett–Koehler
Publishers

Berrett-Koehler is an independent publisher dedicated to an ambitious mission: *Connecting people and ideas to create a world that works for all.*

We believe that the solutions to the world's problems will come from all of us, working at all levels: in our organizations, in our society, and in our own lives. Our BK Business books help people make their organizations more humane, democratic, diverse, and effective (we don't think there's any contradiction there). Our BK Currents books offer pathways to creating a more just, equitable, and sustainable society. Our BK Life books help people create positive change in their lives and align their personal practices with their aspirations for a better world.

All of our books are designed to bring people seeking positive change together around the ideas that empower them to see and shape the world in a new way.

And we strive to practice what we preach. At the core of our approach is Stewardship, a deep sense of responsibility to administer the company for the benefit of all of our stakeholder groups including authors, customers, employees, investors, service providers, and the communities and environment around us. Everything we do is built around this and our other key values of quality, partnership, inclusion, and sustainability.

This is why we are both a B-Corporation and a California Benefit Corporation—a certification and a for-profit legal status that require us to adhere to the highest standards for corporate, social, and environmental performance.

We are grateful to our readers, authors, and other friends of the company who consider themselves to be part of the BK Community. We hope that you, too, will join us in our mission.

A BK Life Book

BK Life books help people clarify and align their values, aspirations, and actions. Whether you want to manage your time more effectively or uncover your true purpose, these books are designed to instigate infectious positive change that starts with you. Make your mark!

To find out more, visit **www.bkconnection.com**.

Berrett–Koehler
Publishers

Connecting people and ideas
to create a world that works for all

Dear Reader,

Thank you for picking up this book and joining our worldwide community of Berrett-Koehler readers. We share ideas that bring positive change into people's lives, organizations, and society.

To welcome you, we'd like to offer you a free e-book. You can pick from among twelve of our bestselling books by entering the promotional code **BKP92E** here: http://www.bkconnection.com/welcome.

When you claim your free e-book, we'll also send you a copy of our e-news-letter, the *BK Communiqué*. Although you're free to unsubscribe, there are many benefits to sticking around. In every issue of our newsletter you'll find

- A free e-book
- Tips from famous authors
- Discounts on spotlight titles
- Hilarious insider publishing news
- A chance to win a prize for answering a riddle

Best of all, our readers tell us, "Your newsletter is the only one I actually read." So claim your gift today, and please stay in touch!

Sincerely,

Charlotte Ashlock
Steward of the BK Website

Questions? Comments? Contact me at bkcommunity@bkpub.com.

MIX
Paper from
responsible sources
FSC® C016245
www.fsc.org

Certified

Corporation
bcorporation.net